DAD NOW WORKIN[...]
FACTORY IN ELIZA[...]
MOVE THERE IN 56

INTO 51 KNIGHTON ROAD BRAND NEW
SEMI DETACHED SA HOUSING COMMISSION
HOME NEXT DOOR, ENNIS FAMILY, PAULA,
OTHER SIDE 'ETSA' LAND VACANT (BUT
FOR SUBSTATION.!!) TURN TO "SHOPS"
FORD CONSUL CAR IN DRIVE, DAD
BUYS + BUILDS GARAGE (IRON)
WALK TO WOMMA STATION CATCH TRAIN
TO GAWLE HIGH SCHOOL 4YRS PHOTO AFTER SIX
BREIF TIME IN E. SOUTH PRIMARY ON BIKE

12 YEARS OLD BECOMING A 'TEENAGER'
NEW AMERICAN WORD DESCRIBING
KEEN FOLLOWER OF R^R CULTURE
· KEEN TEEN " MUSIC + TELEVISON
BECOME LIFE BLOOD ALONG WITH CARS
FILMS (MOVIES GIRLS!!
SCHOOL FRIENDS IAN DOWNER DAVID PENDLEBURY MICK HOLP
JOHN BETTEMAN JANICE SLATER MAUREEN BOND
E. NORTH FRIENDS. MIKE SYKES ANN
CLEM PADDY McCARTNEY 'SPRINGY (TV)
EMMA (WHG SCHOOL) BRIAN HOUGH

GLENN SHORROCK

Glenn Shorrock

THE AUTOBIOGRAPHY

Now, Where Was I?

My career with the Twilights, Axiom
& Little River Band and back again

NEW
HOLLAND

Contents

LRB at the Dallas Cotton Bowl, 1978.

Dedication

'To all those who, by accident or design,

have not been included in this book.'

– Peter Ustinov

Photo: Tony Mott, 2016

Introduction

I've read memoirs that have made me laugh out loud – Stephen Fry comes quickly to mind, as does Spike Milligan and, more recently, Alan Bennett. Peter Ustinov's *Dear Me*, which is a tour de force, is another favourite. These are the great raconteurs of modern times and masters of creative writing, in entertaining and informing the reader. It's an impossible standard, I know, for my own feeble efforts but I am heartened by the fact that this memoir is not intended to be a literary masterpiece. It's just my say on my life and I think I tell it quite honestly, as I remember it.

The big question has always been, could I become a literary person and complete a book on my own? I've always considered myself as a writer and have been encouraged often enough by my wife, friends and music colleagues to write my story.

I must admit, however, that I find being both self-critical and reflective very difficult. As my song 'Will You Stand With Me? states:

The pen has to hit the paper,
an' the notes must strike a chord,
when conditions all seem perfect,
imagination wields the sword.

LRB 1976.
(Courtesy Bob King)

The hardest part of writing is staring at the blank page – just the fact that I have a whole life to write down in longhand was daunting enough. I love technology but it does not love me. When I decided to write this memoir I thought it would be a good idea to use the latest tool available, one which digitally translates normal handwriting into text. Perfect for a non-typist like me, right? $1500 later this is the first paragraph I've produced.

I knew I couldn't possibly type it all on computer so I kept on putting it off until the next time … and the next time. I wrote in various notebooks over many years and didn't get very far with it but really, it's thanks to the persistence of those closest to me who said I had to get this down on paper before it's all forgotten.

I often had writer's block writing songs – I probably have it right now – but then I've never been an overly prolific writer. I have 2000 ideas for songs, of course – all of them unfinished – but then my creative life has always been something of a mess.

I am a bit of a dreamer – creative driftwood, I call it. But I'm hard on myself. It's in my nature. I'm the singer, the salesman of the band; that's what I've always been … that's my job. But I can be a lazy bugger too. I understand the effort and the philosophy behind it all but in practice I perhaps goof off too much and am easily distracted.

To write memoirs one should have some memories, right? Well, obviously I have memories, but I was concerned the ones I could actually remember would only fill a pamphlet or brochure; but a whole book?

Start the book! Today!

And that's it! That's the sign I've been looking for. A shaft of sunlight from a Sydney dawn has bathed a small pile of books in my bedroom … not quite the same as those sunlight occurrences in Machu Picchu or the Great Pyramid of Cheops etc. that illuminate mystical symbols of early deities. But all things being relative (according to that famous Austrian scientist), life happens under that same sun, so that's profound enough for me.

I roll over and begin to think of the usual diversions, but as I watch the square of golden sunlight track across the flat-screen

TV topped with cables, the many DVD boxes and onto my wife's framed photographs of family and friends, I know I can delay it no longer.

Start the book! Now!

Am I really able to let all the cats out of the bag, as such? We'll see.

At the end of the day I hope that you, dear reader, will have a better understanding of the bloke who sings the songs you like. I have always thought of myself as a man of the people – I don't think I've been an elitist, except perhaps accidentally, because after a while you get used to being recognised, getting a good seat at a restaurant or joining those clubs we all talk about once we 'make it', but I certainly never set out to be like that; just to be a good entertainer and give good service.

So, read on and I trust you'll enjoy the pages within. It's a good story.

Now, where was I?

My wife Jo and I.
Enjoy!

CHAPTER 1

The Ghost of LRB

So let's begin at the halfway point. On 17 October 2004, the Little River Band was inducted into the ARIA (Australian Record Industry Awards) Hall of Fame. The classic line-up of the band – Graeham Goble, Beeb Birtles, Derek Pellicci, David Briggs, George McArdle and yours truly, Glenn Barrie Shorrock – reunited onstage to accept the award. 'Thank you for inviting us to your party,' I started, making the point that the award was some consolation for certain disappointments we had recently suffered.

The reunion is going so well, I said, we can't keep our hands off each other.

It was forty years almost to the day since we had met in London with manager Glenn Wheatley with the idea of forming a new band. Then, for the first time in more than twenty-five years, this line-up took part in a live performance of 'Help Is On Its Way' as a finale to a memorable night.

Getting together for the ARIAs was a bittersweet occasion, somewhat awkward for certain individuals, but a welcome one I think for all involved. We put any past differences we may have had to one side because of the importance of the occasion and just enjoyed ourselves. Various other members of the band – John Farnham, Wayne Nelson, Steve Housden and the current nameless players performing under the LRB banner in the US – were not included in the ceremony.

The classic Little River band line-up: (from left) Beeb Birtles, Graeham Goble, Derek Pellicci, George McArdle, Glenn Shorrock and David Briggs. Ready to take on the world!

The ridiculous irony about this big moment was we had to secure a twenty-four hour 'licence' from the owner of the LRB 'trademark' in order to perform that song as Little River Band. How did we ever get to that point?

There were five key people who were constants in the success of LRB – Graeham, Beeb, Derek, myself and manager Glenn Wheatley. Everyone else in the band revolved around that core, coming in and out of the band like a revolving door.

The problem is, Little River Band – an Australian band of which I was a foundation member, that broke into the American charts; a band that I named after a country town outside Geelong, and then fronted during the group's halcyon days – never officially broke up. Never one of the more stable musical line-ups, LRB's key members were either 'replaced' (me, twice!), sacked, let go or simply walked away from it.

Instead of turning the lights off, last man standing Stephen

On stage for the ARIA Hall of Fame in 2004 after thirty years – David, me, George, Beeb, Derek and Graeham – LRB, back together for one night only ... literally!

Housden, who joined the group in 1981, continued on. Boosted by the return of Wayne Nelson, our third bass player, who had first joined the band in 1980, Housden filled the band with sound-alike (and in my case, look-alike) session players and continued performing under the LRB name and famous platypus logo.

Housden does not even perform with the band anymore; he allows the current line-up to use the name Little River Band while denying us the opportunity to perform with any reference to our time in the band. The 'current' LRB tours the US for six to eight months a year, turning over about a million dollars annually. It's a lucrative gig.

This all became clear to the original members of the band when, early in the new millennium, we put aside years of infighting and committed ourselves to putting the band back together again.

Graeham Goble had been contacted by a promoter named Paul Roger, a 'fan with a plan' who ran a production company called Stream AV. The project was energetically driven by Graeham, who was keen to remedy past misjudgments and reclaim the band's legacy. He contacted Beeb and me to see if we would be interested in performing again with the 'classic' line-up of Goble, Birtles, Pellicci, Briggs, McArdle and me. It was 2001, at the start of a new century. Why not!

The plan was to tour as the 'Original Little River Band', and when Glenn Wheatley became involved we were sure that we would land dates in the US as well. That's when Stephen Housden and his lawyers came calling.

As the sole director of We Two Pty Ltd, the company that controlled LRB, Housden issued an injunction preventing us from performing under that name. How could that happen? The ensuing court case in June 2002 revealed just how naive the original members of the band had been.

According to lawyers, the business side of LRB had been 'a shambles' at times. In 1975, we had formed a trading company called Little River Band Pty Ltd, which was the legal owner of the LRB name and associated trademarks. The band members who were shareholders in this company were the guys on stage at the ARIAs.

George McArdle left the band in 1979, David Briggs was replaced by Stephen Housden in 1981 and I was replaced by John Farnham the following year. Beeb left in 1983 and, following the release of the 1986 album *No Reins*, LRB stopped touring and severed ties with manager Glenn Wheatley and with Capitol Records.

In 1988, the year after LRB had reformed with me as lead singer and was signed by MCA, the band's trademarks were transferred to a 'clean slate' company called We Two Pty Ltd ('We Two' being a Graeham Goble song from 1983). The problem was, the new company did not include the original members of the band, rather the then line-up of Graeham Goble, Derek Pellicci, Wayne Nelson, Stephen Housden and me. Goble left the band in 1989 and Wayne Nelson in 1993, although he returned two years later. Are you keeping up?

According to Beeb, he did not even know that the legal transfer of said trademarks had occurred, having not been asked to re-join the band.

My own situation was slightly different. When push came to shove in 1996 and I couldn't continue on the next LRB tour, I was told by legal representatives that it was two (Housden and Pellicci) against one and so, for a second time in the band's history, I was replaced by another singer. I was later awarded $80,000 as compensation for loss of earnings after being dropped from the 1996 US tour.

The following year, Derek quit the band for personal reasons, leaving Housden in full control of the company which owns LRB, a situation that continues to this day.

As ex-directors of the company that owned the LRB trading name, or 'brand' as it is now known, Beeb, Graeham and I launched a high court challenge against Stephen Housden with a view to us touring once more under the LRB banner. Thousands in legal bills later, the outcome of the case hinged on whether Glenn Wheatley and Graeham Goble had signed a document relinquishing their ownership of the LRB name. It was asserted that they did not do this.

The Federal Court case in Melbourne was fairly brutal. The constant personnel changes over the years had confused audiences but the important thing was the ownership of the trademarked name, including its abbreviation, and the band's distinctive logo. LRB's then agent Steve Green, the President of International Artists Management which handled the band's tour schedule, said 'the songs drew the audiences, not the band members'.

What?

We wanted to tour as the 'original' LRB, but this would have been confusing with the 'current' LRB also touring at the same time. In an affidavit quoted in court by Housden's lawyers, Graeham Goble stated that he believed 'we would not be able to identify to the public who we are' without using the name LRB.

Justice Ray Finkelstein knew the history of such music business disputes, citing cases regarding the ownership of the Inkspots and the Kingsmen. The Inkspots started out as a vocal group in the 1930s before becoming a doo-wop band in the 1950s and are still touring the US, after obvious personnel changes. The Kingsmen only had one major hit, the garage band classic 'Louie, Louie', but various line-ups of the band had to fight for the right to carry the name on tour.

There are many other examples too, of course; the lasting bitterness over ownership of the name Pink Floyd that led to the falling out between Dave Gilmour and Roger Waters is only one. Bloody hell!

Just when it looked like we might win the court case, we were informed that the missing document confirming the transfer or the LRB name had been found in a box in Florida. It was only a copy, the original couldn't be found, but there it was with Wheatley's and Goble's signature on it.

A settlement was reached that prevented the three of us from using the name Little River Band or its trademark abbreviation or logo in any re-formation we might be involved in. The 'reality' was we *were* the original members of the band but we had to tread carefully how we marketed ourselves so as not to infringe on their copyright ownership.

Suffice to say, some of us had taken our eyes off the ball and mistakes had been made that would cause much frustration and anger over the following years. I can't say that I'm entirely blameless in all this but the others bear much more culpability because they were not 'let go' like I had been and, remember, I came up with the bloody name!

Promoter Paul Rodger believed that Birtles, Shorrock and Goble could still form a band around our heritage, being the main writers of the LRB songs and the combined 'voice' of the band, so plans were drawn up for a 'BSG' tour. I thought it sounded like an accounting firm but, what the hell, in for a penny in for a pound.

Graeham had been demo-ing songs with Michael Costa, Paul's partner at Stream AV, which brought new musicians into play as a backing band. Graeham always had a very good sense of who was willing to work for the greater glory! They included Jason Vorherr on bass, Simon Hosford on guitar, Dave Beck on drums and Dorian West on anything, but mainly keyboard, and a passionate percussionist named Alejandro Vega. I loved working with these guys and they gave the LRB repertoire great value.

Rather than being a joyful LRB reunion, I saw the Birtles Shorrock Goble project as just another job. The bitterness of the past dissipated, however, and Birtles Shorrock Goble worked well together. Today, I don't carry any grudge with those guys about the way things turned out. I also have a good relationship

Back in LRB in 1988 at the launch of the *Monsoon* album. From left, Derek, Graeham, me, Wayne Nelson and Steve Housden. Where's Beeb? He says he was never invited back ...

with Glenn Wheatley; we sit and remember the good times and there's no finger pointing about what happened in LRB.

But I'm not the innocent twenty-one year old who left Adelaide with my mates in a pop band in the 1960s, all of us happily naive. I've got the scars of battle as it were; the music business and the backstabbing hardens you, so you need to be tough otherwise you get taken advantage of.

And LRB played a definite role in that hardening; worse than a divorce, being replaced in the band in 1982 was my first major real-life crisis. I just didn't see that coming. There were mumblings of course and the other guys seemed dissatisfied with the way I was conducting myself within the structure of LRB. But I'm not confrontational; I'll go back inside my shell and internalise issues – real head in the sand stuff – and walk away from it.

Back in 2005, Paul Rodger was trying to give the project some impetus and direction but Graeham Goble and Glenn Wheatley joined forces again and I was confused about just who was in charge. There was money to be made from the private and corporate events but it was clear the general public wanted the original band performing as LRB, not BSG.

Although Glenn Wheatley took over the management of BSG from him, Paul Rodger was interested in producing a DVD and accompanying CD along the lines of the Eagles' 'Hell Freezes Over' tour. In 2005, Birtles Shorrock Goble recorded a successful DVD and live CD called *Full Circle*.

BSG scored some great gigs over the next couple of years, including the Grand Prix Ball in 2003 and the AFL grand final, and the thirtieth anniversary *Countdown* concert tour in 2006, on which we 'represented' LRB. We did other private functions and

There's Beeb! Birtles Shorrock and Goble in the early 2000s ... good to be back together but not quite LRB. (Courtesy Bob King)

charity balls but LRB's legal team in Florida were keen to catch us out and we had to be careful of crossing the legal minefields.

It was not so much that the ghost of LRB was haunting us, more that we had become the ghost of LRB.

We stayed together for a few years, but logistically the three key members were all over the place so it was always difficult to coordinate a tour. Because of the problems with promoting the gigs – we couldn't have Little River Band or LRB in any promotional material – we only played 'the big stuff' rather than mounting a full-scale tour of Australia.

Fast-forward to more than a decade after the ARIA award and in January 2015 I was informed by several fans that the current LRB had been booked on the top-rating US *Tonight Show* hosted by Jimmy Fallon. The promos were saying that LRB was celebrating their fortieth anniversary as a band and would be singing 'their' hits including 'Reminiscing'.

Hang on!

I decided to stir things up a little by sending an email to the producers of the *Tonight Show.* I pointed out to them that *that* LRB line-up was not forty years old at all and were not entitled to that claim. In fact, they were 'grinding our good name into the dust' by their constant touring and false promotion. The Fallon show were also using clips of *our* performances to promote the name 'LRB'. That was just a bridge too far for me ...

After outlining my 'disgust and outrage' I signed off with, 'If you do decide to put them on the show just pass on my message to go fuck yourselves.' The press, of course, reported that I had told Fallon to fuck himself, but not true. The missive had the desired effect though, making headlines on both sides of the Pacific. In the end it was Graeham Goble's publisher who was able to block LRB from performing his songs live on TV and their appearance on the *Tonight Show* was abruptly cancelled.

I liken the current LRB to a tribute band but I don't begrudge them touring or want to stop them from playing our music.

I also don't gloat about the fact that the current LRB can't tour here with their line-up either, not because of any court injunction, but because they would struggle to draw a crowd. Everyone is entitled to make a living but don't pretend that you are us and use promotional images from the original band to earn your living. That's not playing fair.

In the years since then, the anger over what happened to us has subsided because the music of LRB still is popular around the world and I will always remain the voice of the band. My workload hasn't diminished; in fact, I'm financially better off now than ever but that's not the issue.

As a foundation member of the group, I have a bit of objectivity about it all now; we did bloody well as a band, selling over 30 million units, but we were fairly well down the totem pole of 'great' bands. I believe I was always a good team player, however, and loyal to the other members of LRB. But I will always have that sense of betrayal with me, and the added regret that the band did not reach its full potential because of the mistakes we made.

My history with Little River Band is carried sometimes heavily, sometimes lightly, on my shoulders but it's never that far away from me. The angst over the loss of our ability to perform as LRB is driven by various supporters of both camps, who seem more interested than me, sometimes, about what went down. And boy do they get upset!

I'm proud of LRB and what we achieved but I have a lot of emotions about my years in the band – happiness, sadness, disappointment, anger – and I would gladly leave it all in the past if LRB would leave me alone. There's always someone out there who wants to revive the conflict or bankroll a new tour but does anyone really care anymore?

The current owners of the Little River Band 'brand' have thwarted my efforts to perform in America but I'm just not prepared to fight them in the US legal system because it's too

Jo and I in our comfort zone. No, I don't have a headache ... I just often look like this.
(Courtesy Simon Kenny)

22

expensive. I believe I could win but I'd be bankrupt by the process. I enjoy my life here in Oz too much and I want to keep performing if and when the opportunity arises. Today, 'Trumpland' has little appeal to me. I'll take plain old 'Turnbullville' any day.

The ghost of LRB will always be there but it's not the whole story.

It's not my whole story.

CHAPTER 2

The Boy Shorrock

Now, where was I? Ah yes, the beginning. I was born during the War in '44, pulled from the rubble of a German blitz.

Great beginning that, lad, though not entirely true. My mother, however, still reminds me that I was placed in the bottom of a chest of drawers for protection during the final year of World War II. Hitler was becoming increasingly desperate and sent pilotless rockets across Kent to fall on London. Some didn't make it that far and fell on us during those terrifying times. So, my life began just as the war was reaching a welcome but brutal conclusion, although, almost seventy-five years later, the world is no closer to achieving peace.

There is a lovely caption on the back of this photo that says, 'The boy Shorrock'. That's me playing with a straight bat wearing my father's cricket kit (he was, after all, a Yorkshireman!) From the size of the pads, which came up to my stomach, the chance of lbw had increased considerably.

Joyce and Harry Shorrock saw fit to beget me into this world, having lost their first child at birth. I was born in Chatham Hospital in Kent, England, and soon after was taken to the family home in Rochester, the first of the three 'Medway Towns' on the way east out of London, alongside Chatham and Gillingham.

My father Harry Shorrock was born in Wakefield, in South Yorkshire, and grew up in the small town of Earby, the youngest sibling of Mabel, Tom and Fred. When we would visit there, we always stayed with Fred and his wife Florrie on the edge of town, bordering farms on the Yorkshire moors. Young Harry soon found he could make things and did so fashioning toys for children using his newfound carpentry skills. He liked exercise in the form of boxing and weightlifting 'and such', and encouraged me to follow suit (with little success).

Just before the war, and following his involvement in a fatal motorbike accident, which was never talked about, Harry Shorrock went down to Kent. There he met and married Joyce Smith, and reluctantly became part of the slightly bonkers Smith family. My father worked on barrage balloons at Rochester aerodrome, which was often bombed by the Germans in the ensuing years. A conscientious objector to the war, Dad served in the home guard and his did his bit on the home front as part of the million-strong 'Dad's Army'.

My mother's family were always an important part of my childhood. My 'Nanny' worked in the Two Brewers pub in High Street, which was run by my uncle, John Taylor, who had married Madeline, my mother's 'glamorous' older sister. Uncle John was a large, jolly man who later became my favourite benefactor.

My grandmother was a tiny, formidable, grumpy old lady who I didn't care for too much (she smelled of liniment and Craven A cigarettes). Her demeanor was probably caused by the departure of my grandfather for Washington (USA) before I was born. Nanny Smith ran a boarding house in a lane opposite the pub for itinerant workers arriving during the war from parts northern, one of whom was a handsome, balding Yorkshireman named Harry Shorrock. Harry met Joyce and bingo, I was born on 30 June, 1944.

Uncle John and Aunty Mad, as she was known, had a 'posh' house on Watling Street in Strood, on the other side of the Medway River. It was termed a bungalow but to me was a rather grand American-style, bay-windowed house in which they lived with 'Uncle' Bert, who was their 'lodger' (nudge, nudge; wink, wink; say no more – and we didn't). Bert and John doted on Madeline, who was the dominant one in a three-way relationship of which I was pretty much ignorant until very much later in life.

'Little Lord Fauntleroy,' aged 2 (or is it 22?)

Having no children of their own, John and Mad (and Bert) doted on me. In 1950, my sister Lynda came along and our aunts and uncles were extremely kind to Lynda and myself. By this stage I was six, and full of the joys of a childhood in a post-War Britain that was entering the 'new atomic age'.

There was a function room upstairs of the hotel where our family Christmases were celebrated and where everybody 'did a turn'. Dad would have a shandy and recite 'Albert and the Lion' or sing 'Jerusalem'. He had more 'front' and talent than any of us but I soon caught on.

Dad made us all laugh. 'Ooh, Harry,' Mum would join in, 'Stop it.' He was a no-nonsense Yorkshireman so he wasn't a total pussycat, just your typical, 1950s model father. 'Harry played with a straight bat,' they would say (in a broad Yorkshire accent). 'He weren't hitting across the line of the ball!'

Mum and Dad didn't drink; Mum only went to the pub on High Street to entertain me. She would take me inside to show me off to the customers. 'Ooh, he's a lovely boy, Joyce,' the customers would say. 'Ooh, look at him. Where did you get him from?' Mum put me behind the bar and I would sell packets of crisps thinking I was really grown up. 'Tuppence please, mister.'

Uncle John was also a local entrepreneur in downtown Rochester and managed the local roller-skating rink, which also doubled as the dance hall. The Locarno Ballroom was frequented often by Mum and Dad, who were very good at ballroom dancing; well I thought so, as I watched them glide across the floor. John would book bands from London, among them Ted Heath and his Music, and other popular outfits of the day, so we certainly weren't short of a social life.

The Shorrocks, me age 10 and Lynda 4, wearing their finest. No, I am not singing to her but that's a nice bow tie I'm wearing.

Mum's middle sister Phyllis lived in Drewstead Cottage on Streatham Common in South London with her husband Herbert Randall and their sons, Phillip and Geoffrey. My two older cousins were a great influence on me growing up, especially Geoffrey. The two of us would roam across the commons with Dusky, his trusty Alsatian. Geoff had a keen interest in all things 'modern' and dabbled in photography, showing off his imagination and talents producing tableaus of space voyages on black velvet with sugar 'stars' and paper model rocket ships helped, of course, by me.

Holidays were spent with my cousins Geoff and Philip in London or with Uncle John, Aunty Mad and Bert camping on farms in Devon and Cornwall. On those holidays in Drewstead Cottage, I shared the upstairs bedroom with Geoff, which was only feet away from the railway line from Victoria Station on the Southern line. Uncle Herbert was an inspector on British Rail so

The Smith sisters: (from left) my mother Joyce, middle sister Phyllis and the 'glamorous' Madeline. Mum was the youngest, but my aunts loomed large in our family legend.

trains were always prominent in our stays with the Randalls. So much so that through the night it often felt like the trains were coming through the bedroom window, but you got used to the constant shaking of the building after a while.

My memories of these early days in England are hazy now, of warm hospitality and tea in cold Victorian mill workers' cottages. Of bonfire nights and blacksmiths! Of playing around World War II wrecks and almost falling in a moat surrounding an ammo depot. One memory sticks out though; a trip to the 'famous' seaside town of Blackpool and a visit to the iconic tower in which there was a zoo with a lion called Wallace, which inspired the story 'Albert and the Lion', as told with great regularity and hilarity by my dear old dad.

I was a happy-go-lucky child, surrounded by a wonderful array of adult characters, all slightly 'left of field' and eccentric. I was gregarious and made friends easily, enjoying every day at school. I was never a sportsman; I was the guy who ran 100 yards of the cross-country run then hid behind the toilets before joining in at the end.

My life quickly filled with school days and long summers playing in the woods across the road with my friends Peter and Wendy Lowe and a girl named Topsy, who vied for my affection. But my eyes were only for Wendy, who became Maid Marian to my Robin Hood, Jane to my Tarzan.

The Lowe and Shorrock families were neighbours in Valley View Road, (there was no view to speak of!), which was the centre of my social life, such as it was, as a boy.

I listened to the BBC *Light Programme* on the radio and my favourites, such as *Dick Barton – Special Agent, Educating Archie, Life With The Lyons* and *Take It From Here*. I was also sucked into the sci-fi adventure of *Journey Into Space*.

The Goon Show on UK radio was always eagerly awaited, and their humour is something I have always appreciated and cherished. Peter Sellers has always been an influence on me.

His 1962 film *Only Two Can Play* is one of my favourites, with Sellers musing on his lot as a meek Welsh librarian while he gazes at his bedroom wallpaper patterned with stags, longing for more hedonistic diversions before his time runs out.

My childhood was enjoyably normal. After Sunday dinners (always with Yorkshire pudding and apple pie) we would listen to the *Billy Cotton Band Show* featuring the latest hit parade singers and comedians. My father Harry would amuse us with more renditions of Stanley Holloway monologues. I loved to be entertained.

We would often visit Auntie Mad and Uncle John over the river Medway and listen to their radiogram. They had 78 rpm records by Frank Sinatra, Bing Crosby, Dean Martin and the new sensation, Johnny Ray who was on top of the charts with 'Cry'. Dad preferred opera singers like Caruso, Gigli and the like and would sing operatic arias in pidgin Italian.

I wasn't that interested in music then although I sang the old English air 'Early One Morning' in the classroom choir at St Margaret's Primary. Later, my ear was taken by melodies sung by the crooners of the day on radio, and I took specific notice of Frankie Lane's 'Ghost Riders In The Sky', 'The Ballad of Davy Crockett' by Fess Parker, and Roy Rogers' 'A Four Legged Friend', a song about the love of his faithful horse Trigger, although my real interest was in checking out the great shirts he wore.

In those pre-adolescent days of the 1950s, radio was 'king' but television was a threat to the throne. I was thrilled when I learnt that the Lowe's family had just bought the first television in our street. We were allowed to watch *Muffin The Mule*, *Andy Pandy* and the *Flower Pot Men* after school and then, 'home for tea children!'

My real interests lay in boys' own pursuits like racing cars, jet planes and Wendy!

As I grew up, I came under the spell racing car drivers such as Stirling Moss and Juan Manuel Fangio. My 'Uncle' Bert once took

My fascination with cowboys and Western movies was fully realised in dress-up games (although I look like a dustman in this photo), monthly treats to the local cinema, old movies on black and white TV, and collecting film annuals. Stick 'em up, 'pardener'! (gratuitous Peter Sellers reference).

me to Brands Hatch circuit to watch Geoff Duke, the then World Motorcycle Champion, in action and got his autograph and oily thumbprint. I was also lucky enough to go to the Farnborough Air Show a couple of times and heard the Hawker Hunter jet fighter break the sound barrier. Boom! Jolly good show chaps!

The 1950s remain a magical time in my memory. Kirk Douglas, Burt Lancaster and Tony Curtis dominated the silver screen; Edmund Hillary and Tenzing Norgay reached the summit on Mount Everest, and Elizabeth was crowned queen, her coronation shown live on black-and-white TV. The *Eagle* comic arrived every week with cutaway drawings of centrefolds of aircraft carriers, locomotives and Vulcan bombers. *Playboy* magazine was never as sexy as the *Eagle*!

England was a boy's paradise, so why did we have to leave? The truth was, Dad didn't get on too well with the rest of the family, which must have made our decision to emigrate that

One of the last pictures
taken of the Shorrocks
before we emigrated
to Australia ... a typical
English family of the
early 1950s.

much easier. He thought there was a life outside of hanging around Mum's 'silly' family and in the end, I think he was glad to get out of there. That was my impression as a boy and, in hindsight, he was portably right.

I didn't take too much notice of my parents pouring over brochures about Canada, New Zealand and Australia. We first considered New Zealand but the quota was full, so Australia it was. Even when I was told we were emigrating it had little effect on me and even less on my four-year-old sister. Of course, it was a huge decision for my parents and Mum had strong reservations about leaving her family. Dad, however, had his way, such was the relationship between husband and wife in those days.

Soon after, father announced to all our family and friends that we were going to leave England for a new life in Australia. In August 1954, the Shorrock family left Kent for the docks at Tilbury on the Thames, with four tea chests packed full of our belongings packed in Bert's van and Madeline's car. We boarded the RMS *Orcades*, of the Orient Line, as 'assisted migrants', bound for our new life in Australia.

It was an emotional time for Mum and my Nanny, and many tears were shed as we bade farewell. But I did not cry. My heart was pumping in anticipation of a great adventure. The four Shorrocks looked down from the promenade deck of the ship as the rest of our family stood on the dock clutching streamers, in one last flimsy connection to our old life. My hands gripping the ship's railings suddenly felt the vibrations of the engines turning over and, with a blast from the funnel, we set sail into the Thames estuary, snapping the streamers and breaking the link to Mother England.

Or so we thought!

CHAPTER 3

The Odyssey

Passengers on board the *Orcades* were divided into first class and tourist class, a slight misnomer because tourist class consisted almost wholly of migrants travelling on assisted passage. Provided by the Australian Government of the day, we were 'ten-pound Poms', referring to the small amount we had to pay up-front to secure our passage to Australia and our new life. The real tourists were in first class paying their own way. They were rarely seen strolling past our rooms but they occupied three quarters of the ship, including all the upper decks.

We found ourselves on 'D' deck – 'D' for dangerous, or dingy – but luckily, we had our own four-berth cabin, albeit with no window and the port propeller shaft shuddering through the night as our next-door neighbour. I later made some friends on board including a snotty-nosed Scot whose name I've forgotten. We managed to infiltrate first class for all of two minutes before being marched back to cattle class by an officer soon striped with little 'Jocks' snot.

Children were served dinner at 5.30 pm and mothers could accompany us. Then adults were served in two sittings. My first meal went unnoticed as my eyes were glued to the first part of our journey rounding the Kent coast, past our favourite day trip seaside town of Margate, and on down the channel. With France on the left and England on the right, our home gradually disappeared in the distance as we steamed into the Bay of Biscay,

Me, age 5, sporting a look of mischief and the original Beatles haircut (and this is in 1950!). I later used this image on the cover of my 2007 album *Meanwhile … Acoustically*. Would you trust this boy?

where the real fun began.

The Bay of Biscay is a notorious stretch of water on the edge of the Atlantic prone to storms and large seas. Sleep was impossible that first night as we clung to the iron bunks as the *Orcades* pitched and rolled and shuddered as the props came out of the water and back in again, sending the shafts into spasms.

Breakfast the next morning was hilarious, once we made it up the flights of stairs and gangways to the dining room. Everything was in constant motion; food, diners and waiters all joining in a symphony of mayhem. Yes, the sea was angry that day my friends, as were the waiters trying to serve the meal. What fun! Food and plates sliding everywhere. Someone managed to grab a piece of toast or boiled egg as they flew down the table past us, as did the waiters. Faces were either etched in laughter (us) or terror (them) but I tried to look like I had been doing this all my life until I speared my thigh with a fork and watched my sausage roll onto another boy's plate some twenty feet away. After a couple of days at sea things calmed down somewhat and my family soon made friends and settled down to share experiences, good and bad.

Geography being my best subject at school, I was always well-informed and opinionated as to my place on the surface of the planet, as I am still to this day. I studied the map of our itinerary

A scene from one of my favourite films, Hitchcock's *The Birds*! Although this clearly features Australian birds, by the look of our school uniforms I think this photo was taken at a zoo in England. My sister looks absolutely petrified.

daily, charting our progress, distance travelled and places to visit. In the 1950s, the map of the world still had a significant degree of pink, representing the British Empire, and most of our stops were at places still under British influence.

Gibraltar was our first 'foreign' port of call; the famous British outpost sitting at the southern end of Spain at the entrance to the Mediterranean. 'The Rock' looks across the straits of the same name toward Algeria and Morocco. The town itself clings to a narrow strip of land that almost joins the rock to Spain and offered the visitor a mixture of Spanish and English culture – fish and chips with olives and salsa!

The other feature of our brief stay was encountering the Barbary apes that live on the rock and which were not shy in coming forward for a share of aforesaid fish and chips, to the horror of my sister. Some were quite large and aggressive and we left there with many stories of minor injuries, mayhem and theft at the hands of the exotic inhabitants.

Back on board the *Orcades*, life settled down and the Mediterranean Sea did the same as we cruised towards Naples, Italy. We passengers took on the look of a seal colony, albeit pink seals flecked with black soot from the exhaust from the ship's funnel. A film was shown at the back deck once a week and I especially enjoyed the original *Blue Lagoon*, which would have a lasting effect on me, and *The Crimson Pirate* starring the great Burt Lancaster.

I was soon relishing the adventure of overseas voyaging. The warm sun of the 'Med' was our constant companion and the swimming pool was finally opened! The entrance of the aft luggage hold was sealed off and filled with seawater and quickly became our Lido and my domain.

'See Naples and die' was a popular phrase bandied on board the ship as we got closer to our destination. I soon realised it meant see Naples and die happy! We arrived at Naples in the shadow of the famous volcano Mount Vesuvius. Not surprisingly, this was the first volcano I had ever seen and I was somewhat disappointed that it was not erupting. All was quiet, except for some steam and smoke escaping from its cone. I watched it for ages through my binoculars, given to me by my dear Uncle John for my journey, and was in awe of its majestic presence.

Some of the crew were Neapolitans and told us about their hometown and what to expect, especially in regard to the ruins of Pompeii on the southern flank of the volcano. I nagged Mum and Dad to take me on the organised tour and we set off in the less than salubrious bus on the ninety-minute journey to Pompeii, with a visit to a cameo factory on the way for the purchase of souvenirs (obviously the commercial part of the tour!).

The ancient city of Pompeii had been devastated by the volcano in Roman times (79 AD) but in 1950s it was in the process of being excavated. The ancient city was buried under a huge pyroclastic flow of superheated ash and rock that incinerated its inhabitants and left them entombed for hundreds of years. One of the morbid features of our visit was being shown the casts of bodies, as they fell under tonnes of ash. Over the centuries, their bodies had completely decayed, leaving the space surrounded by volcanic material. Archaeologists filled the spaces left with plaster, revealing the human forms of the fallen, in the final throes of agony.

It was an amazing experience and one I shall never forget. The power of nature and Mother Earth has fascinated me ever since. I hung onto every word that our guide uttered as we spent two hours walking the well-preserved Roman ruins, villas, etc. with chariot 'ruts' clearly visible and amphitheatres where gladiator events took place. There's nothing like a good natural disaster to excite a young mind.

We sailed south-east past the Isle of Capri and steamed into the Suez Canal. I remember sighting the coast of Egypt in the first light of day, already sensing how hot the day was going to be. Port Said, pronounced 'Sy-eed', on the north coast of Egypt

and at the entrance of the canal, was my first taste of the 'Third World' and it was a strange taste to savour.

There was a great hubbub of activity at Port Said. The hull of the ship was surrounded by what were known as 'bumboats', hawkers in small dinghies competing with each other selling local trinkets and souvenirs and calling out to us above, peering down over the railings. 'McGregor, McGregor!' they yelled. It seemed all Brits were known by that name.

Magicians came on board and enthralled us with uncanny tricks and illusions, such as pulling live chicks from thin air or better still, the ear of an unsuspecting child. He was called the 'Gully Gully Man' and he had us all spellbound with his tricks.

Once a hawker attached themselves to an interested customer the bargaining would begin. A rope with a weight on one end was thrown up by the hawker from his boat so the artefacts and trinkets could be passed up from the bumboat to the deck. If a price was agreed to, the money was lowered down to the boat in the same manner.

The gangplank was lowered soon after and we all went ashore to run the gauntlet of street sellers and to get a feeling for what a real 'foreign country' was like. The street sellers tried to palm their wares – mainly stuffed toy camels and pyramid trinkets – although one of the subtler items also caught my eye. Behind rows of postcards were letters of a 'lewd' nature, although being ten years old, I had no idea what lewd was. The hawker asked my father, 'Do you want to see the donkey and the lady?' which my father quickly declined.

I took it all at face value: 'Who would buy a postcard with a donkey and a lady on it?' I thought to myself, but the real

A lovely photo of a happy couple, Harry and Joyce Shorrock, on their way out for a night's dancing … not so strictly ballroom! Dad hated getting dressed up but he was a handsome man.

situation was later illuminated by the older boys who described in full detail to us young innocents what was on the postcard, the image of which has haunted me ever since.

We found the streets far too intimidating and returned to the boat. The Gully Gully Man was still on board the following morning! So much for security in the fifties! My mother wilted and bought an unstuffed leather 'pouffe' which later became my TV 'poof' when we finally landed in Australia.

Passage through the canal was a surreal experience. I recall visions of ships gliding through sand dunes, shimmering in the heat mirage as we passed them heading north back through the canal. We came into the Red Sea after a day and a half at the town of Suez itself. I had read about this sea from Hans Hass and Jacques Cousteau, the scuba pioneers. The water was still and flat and it was now very hot and so I kept a keen eye out for a shark or some other denizen of the deep. Alas, nothing but the ever-present flying fish.

We steamed into Aden, the southernmost port in the Red Sea, and the temperature rose even more. Nevertheless, we went ashore for a trip to the city, baking in a crater long extinct, but still the heat was volcanic! The most lingering memory of this place was the beggar children, deliberately disfigured to gain even more sympathy! It was a nightmarish vision into human suffering and has stayed with me to this day.

A few days later, Bombay appeared through a beautiful red dawn. India! Land of wonders and endless people. We spent the whole day amongst them, tasting, smelling, marvelling and often disgusted. Dad was particularly disturbed by the constant spitting by the locals of chewed betel nut juice, a mild stimulant I was told. I managed to talk my parents into buying me an ornamental dagger in a carved wooden sheath that became my pride and joy, long lost now. Bombay was an awesome spectacle. A day later we docked in Colombo in Ceylon as it was named then. Again, we were confronted by the 'Third World' but this time we enjoyed a bus tour to a resort called Mount Lavinia, which catered for the 'Ingleesh' with tea and scones, curried of course.

It took ten days and nights to cross the Indian Ocean from the subcontinent to Australia. It felt longer to me, having nothing much to do except eat and swim and gaze out to the never-ending horizon. I was enthralled by the presence of pairs of albatrosses following in the wake of the *Orcades* looking for food. These magnificent birds with a nine-feet wingspan soared for hours on our stern. I was made aware that they spend 80 per cent of their lives navigating the oceans of the world like this. Immortalised in the poem *The Rime Of The Ancient Mariner* by Samuel Taylor Coleridge, I later managed to include a reference to them in the lyrics of my song 'Cool Change' some twenty-five years later.

On 4 September 1954, I passed from the Northern to the Southern Hemisphere for the first time in my life, an experience I was to have many more times in the future. My sister Lynda and I were willing participants in the slapstick equator ceremony, marked with flour and water and offal with a certificate to admit us to Neptune's realm! The only land we saw was the Cocos Islands, a series of coral atolls miles from anywhere and an old British dominion, now back in the news at the time of writing trying to further their aim to join closer to Australia culturally and economically.

Over the horizon and far away, was the Bikini Atoll, famous of course for the atomic bomb testing and swimwear. There was no mushroom cloud to be seen but some evidence of the latter phenomenon around the pool, worn by one glamorous lady, who was already known as 'that scarlet woman'.

Excited anticipation was the mood of us all as we neared Australia. Gangways were narrowed as luggage appeared around the ship marked with Perth tags. We docked at Fremantle in the dead of night and awoke to an oppressively hot September morning. The light was dazzling but the welcoming port was not

- more suited to cargo or livestock arrivals. Once adjusted, the Shorrocks and all on board were keen to stretch our sea legs and greet our new country and we were soon on buses sightseeing around the Swan River city.

I've tried to remember how I felt that first day in Australia, more than sixty years ago. I was only ten years old but I felt a certain energy inside. There was a mixture of very bright sunlight, vivid blue sky and of course, the heat. Something awakened in me on that new morning. My family felt it too I think; anticipation mixed with trepidation and excitement as to what was to come in our lives.

Kings Park overlooking Perth city and the wide Swan River was the strongest visual memory of that day, now reinforced of course by numerous visits to Western Australia throughout my life. One stop on our tour that day was a visit to 'Tudor Court', which I realise now was to ensure that England was still with us new migrants, even if very far away geographically. It still exists amongst the glass towers of today as a sort of Disney World arcade of shops, but you wouldn't compare it to Uluru or the Opera House, would you?

We left Fremantle minus a few people who were settling in Western Australia. Sailing south we turned left at Albany and headed across the Great Australian Bight, a stretch of ocean well known for its turbulence, and it didn't disappoint. Our journey had been largely benign for most of the five weeks, apart from the Bay of Biscay in France, and again the *Orcades* lurched across heavy seas, which excited yours truly but not so many of our fellow travellers. The sound and smell of seasickness was quite evident for those last days at sea my friends.

Unbeknown to me, immigration officials had joined the ship in Perth and announced that there were too many families being settled in Melbourne, where we were originally headed. Would some of us consider disembarking in Adelaide at the next port? For some reason, my parents agreed to do so and our long

In fancy dress as a Roman centurion or an early cross-dresser? I can't recall. The party was in honour of the 21st birthday of my Twilights' bandmate Mike Sykes, conducted in the friendly surrounds of the family garage.

journey across half the globe ended somewhat unceremoniously at Adelaide's outer harbour on 19 September 1954.

Looking back, I was both glad and sad to finish what was the most significant and enjoyable journey of my young life. The Shorrocks said goodbye to the good ship *Orcades* and quickly cleared customs, which I recall was conducted in a long cargo shed like the one in Fremantle.

We had come halfway across the world searching for the Promised Land and found Adelaide.

CHAPTER 4

Adelaide

What I remember most about our new home in the 1950s was just how flat Adelaide was. There was literally nothing there. Finsbury Park Migrant Hostel on Grand Junction Road was our first home in our new country. When we first set eyes on it the hostel looked like a prison, à la the film *Stalag 17*. I half expected William Holden to be making a break for it at any moment.

After such an exciting voyage, the ten-year-old me was somewhat confused as to what we had done to be sent to these spartan surroundings. What had we done wrong? The perimeters were lined with barbed wire and we saw what looked like guard posts on each corner. Thankfully, they turned out to be water tanks. Our home was a corrugated iron Nissen hut – a half cylinder structure lying on its flat side, approximately 20 metres long and divided into two dwellings. Four of these structures surrounded a shared toilet and laundry block and in the centre of the camp was a large hall, also made of corrugated iron, which was the dining room for us 'inmates'.

Needless to say, Mum and Dad were somewhat taken aback by the sparseness of our new reality. Mum's tears flowed and didn't dry up for weeks. My sister Lynda and I were concerned about the state Mum was in but, being kids, we put on our best faces and tried to cheer her up, as did Dad. But I remember it was the cause of a long-running discussion/argument between the two of them that was very stressful.

My attempt at looking like a rocker while wearing my high school uniform in late 1950s' Adelaide. Narrow tie, narrow belt and narrow trousers. That was the fashion of the day.

Me? Like most kids, I was determined to make the best of it. I was pretty adaptable, given the many schools I attended, and I don't think my schooling suffered too much. My geography certainly improved, with English, art and Latin(!) my strong suits. Forget the rest!

I don't remember how many guests were housed as the migrant hostel but it must have been in the hundreds, mostly Brits like us, but also some Dutch, German and various other European nationalities. I soon met another boy of my own age named Alan Gawthorpe and we became firm friends, exploring our new lives together. Alan went on to become a captain for the now defunct Ansett Airlines and he still drops me a line now and then.

I was enrolled in a nearby primary school while my mum began to plan our escape, having endured our first summer in Adelaide when the temperature was 46 degrees Celsius (105 degrees Fahrenheit) on Christmas Day. In early January 1955, the nearby Mount Lofty Ranges went up in flames in one of the state's, and Australia's, worst bushfires. Australia appeared to be a bloody dangerous place!

Many migrants flocked to the beaches to have a paddle. There are few surf beaches in South Australia and very few of us could swim anyway. Semaphore Beach, where we often went for a swim with other families, was so shallow and calm you couldn't help but paddle!

Dad managed to get a job as a fitter and turner with a British aeronautic firm, part of the government's Weapons Research Establishment (which sounded quite impressive to me), in the northern suburb of Salisbury, ten or so miles from the city. We moved into our first 'real' home, renting a semi-detached house in Bagster Road. I began school lessons at Salisbury North primary school.

Mum now had her own house and kitchen but she was still unhappy and homesick for England. Finally, after about six

Dressing up as King
Farouk on one of the
two trips we made
to Australia by ship.
The then despot of
Egypt, Farouk was
very much in the news
at the time and was
an easy target for my
fancy-dress efforts on
board the ship.

months in Australia, Dad decided that Mum and us kids should return to Kent and he would join us once our 'assisted passage' was refunded as per the government contract. Dad would lodge at the home of a co-worker until the fares were repaid and then join us 'back home' some time later.

I didn't know that was part of the contract until much later. I couldn't understand why some Aussies looked down their noses as us ten-pound Poms. 'You didn't pay to come here, you're a ten-pound Pom,' kids would shout at me in the school playground.

'Of course, I didn't pay,' I'd counter. 'My dad paid, so take it up with him.'

It was another tearful goodbye, especially for Lynda and Dad, as we boarded the liner *Strathmore* at Outer Harbour, Adelaide, for our return to England. I recall very little of this journey, except winning first prize in the fancy dress competition as the Egyptian despot King Farouk, helped by a pillow up my shirt and a bona fide fez purchased in Port Said (enough said!).

Uncle John and Nanny were there to welcome the three of us home and we moved in with Nanny in her new home in Strood, across the Medway from Rochester. I found myself in yet another school, Temple Farm secondary, class 1A. The school was divided into four 'houses' named after prominent seafaring captains: Francis, Drake, Raleigh and Grenville. The latter was to be mine.

I sat for and passed the '11 plus' exam for progress into upper school and enjoyed learning, as my report cards confirmed. Just as I was turning twelve and being measured for long trousers, Mum announced we were returning to Australia. Talk about an upheaval ... here we go again! This time we would have to pay our own passage, which was quickly done before I turned twelve and had to pay full fare. Also, to meet our tight budget, we would have to travel on an Italian ship, which left from Germany.

So once more Mum said goodbye to our family and we set off on another adventure. I hadn't noticed before that we had brought a washing machine back with us from Adelaide and now it was being returned to whence it came. It was soon to become the most travelled Hoover single top loader in modern times, rivalling the afore-mentioned Admiral Grenville!

We motored to the port of Harwich in East Anglia and crossed the North Sea to the Hook of Holland then went by train to Bremen, Germany, where we were to board the *Fairstar*. At Bremen station, we left the train but the luggage and Hoover did not. Exhaustion by now had set in and we arrived at a hotel nearby and collapsed into bed under a soft, pillow-like doona. We had never stayed in a hotel nor slept that way before. It was luxury for us.

In the morning, Mum was thankfully informed that the luggage and Hoover had been located and would meet us at the docks for our third voyage to the other side of the world, this time in the company of passengers from northern Europe and a crew of Italians. Stopping at most of the ports visited on my previous voyages, I became much in demand as a guide! After a most enjoyable six-week voyage, I was also able to swear in four or five languages.

The *Fairstar* was part of the Sitmar Line out of Italy and as such was more relaxed than the British ships; a little bit of dolce vita, if you like. Officers socialised with the passengers quite often in the lounges after dinner and I kept a wary eye on a purser officer who seemed to take an interest in my mother. One port on the journey was Marseilles in the south of France and we were able to visit the place where the fictional Count of Monte Cristo was imprisoned. My very own boys' own adventure!

We survived the journey and arrived in Melbourne; our destination, Adelaide, not being on this particular itinerary.

Dad had driven over and met us for a joyous arrival and we drove in his 'new' Ford Consul back to South Australia, having slept the night in the car on the seafront of St Kilda.

Our temporary home was the Elder Park Hostel, situated on the banks of the River Torrens – much different to our previous surroundings – next to the main Adelaide railway station and later the site of the Adelaide Festival Theatre. As it turned out we were only there for a short time, two months or so, but it proved to be an influential period of my life.

I was lying on my bed in my room on another hot day. I was alone and I could hear a radio playing down the corridor. My ear was taken by a sound that was different to anything I'd heard before; it was both primitive and modern at the same time. I rushed down to get a closer listen. When the song finished the announcer said, 'That was "Heartbreak Hotel" by Mr Elvis Presley' and, with a disapproving sigh continued, 'and now it's back to Frank Chacksfield and his orchestra.'

I had heard about this new music called 'rock 'n' roll' through the success of Bill Haley & His Comets, but this was mystical and slightly dangerous. I had to find out more! And so, began my lifelong passion for this exciting new style of music, though I had no idea back then that I would make a career out of it.

Rising to the rank of Flight Sergeant in the Gawler Squadron of Air Training Corps; joining the cadets satisfied my childhood romance with flying and of possibly becoming a test pilot.

Rock, of course, largely evolved from black R&B artists of the 1950s, and even those novelty country songs popular on radio at the time. Elvis led the way because he covered all the bases: 'All Shook Up', 'Don't Be Cruel' and 'Jailhouse Rock'. He dressed like Roy Rogers and sang like a black man, or so they said, but the only black voices I had heard were mainstream stars such as Nat King Cole and Louis Armstrong. So, when I heard Little Richard, Fats Domino and Chuck Berry I was immediately hooked.

When I eventually left school and joined the work force I was introduced to even more influences – even affluence, such as it was – as a junior draftsman-cum-lunch boy. Money provided me with the independence to buy the records I loved. Since those early days, my tastes have become more varied but discerning. The 'effluence' factor also became stronger and I developed what is known as a 'crap detector', especially when it came to the music business.

******

Soon, the Shorrocks were on the move again. Our time in Elder Park had ended and our family fortune had too … almost. We were obliged to find accommodation outside the metropolitan area while we waited for a Housing Commission home from the South Australian government. We moved our meagre belongings, and the Hoover, into a two-room outbuilding on a farm owned by a Mr Jenke in the tiny hamlet of Rowland Flat in the Barossa Valley.

This home had a kitchen on the verandah with a wood-burning stove and a classic outdoor 'dunny' on the banks of a creek. I spent the next four or five months in quite pleasant surroundings, having managed by this time to adjust to all types of conditions. I attended a one-roomed school with seven grades set out in seven rows, and my father drove 50 kilometres to work, to and from, the newly built General Motors Holden car factory while we waited for the next instalment of our adventure.

I happily explored the wine-producing area with my new school chums, some of whom were the sons of the vineyard owners. I also was tasked with bringing Mr Jenke's three cows back from pasture on my way home from school. That was interesting; the only experience I had with cows in England was stepping in their 'muck' (as dad would say), so keeping the cows off the road was quite a struggle. You know how cows are!

We were finally granted a home in the newly built satellite

town of Elizabeth (named after the Queen, no less – just not as palatial at Buckingham Palace) which was being established between Adelaide and Gawler. We moved into our new address, a three-bedroom semi-detached bungalow, at 51 Knighton Road, Elizabeth North. My father had a secure job at Holden, Mum was happy as a housewife again (and would soon get a job in a department store), Lynda began kindergarten and I enrolled in Gawler High School, which was a thirty-minute train ride north (there being no secondary school yet in Elizabeth).

At last we could settle down to a normal existence. Elizabeth was full of other migrant families, mainly British, and there was a good sense of community there. I had my own bedroom and a poster of Elvis went straight up on my wall. It was 1956 and I was twelve years old, American culture had arrived in the form of rock 'n' roll and television. Bliss! I watched all the American shows on our new Astor TV hoping to catch one of my idols in action but of course all we got was Perry Como ('Magic Moments'), Andy Williams ('Moon River') and Guy Mitchell ('Red Feathers') so I absorbed them too. Basically, I became an entertainment junkie and my future was signposted without me knowing it. I was the bastard child of rock 'n' roll.

I also was something of a film fan, which I remain to this day. I loved war movies ... *The Dambusters* with Richard Todd, *Reach For The Stars* with Kenneth More and *Colditz* with John Mills and Dickie Attenborough; historical dramas such as *Quo Vadis*, *Ivanhoe*, *Rob Roy* and *Scaramouche*; musicals such as *Kiss Me Kate*, *Oklahoma!* and *Carousel*; and 'teenager' film such as *Blackboard Jungle* with Glenn Ford and Sidney Poitier, *Rebel Without A Cause* with James Dean and Natalie Wood, and *The Wild One* with Marlon Brando. Not to forget *The Blob* with Steve McQueen!

My time at GHS was a happy one due to my good exam results and a popularity among my fellow students, especially the female variety. One day at lunchtime, I remember two girls coming together and physically vying for my affections ... needless to say, they both won! Sex, cars and rock 'n' roll became my credo; illicit drugs were unknown back then, although I secretly partook in the legal ones, alcohol and tobacco.

The first of that eternal trio was taken to a new level by my next-door neighbour who showed me a thing or two and we lost our virginities. Later in my career, I wrote a song called 'No Full Moon' about that pivotal event. Then there was also an older girl, aged seventeen or so, who coaxed me into 'wagging' school to spend the day with her while she looked after her younger sister when her parents were at work.

The second subject manifested in my hanging out with some older car freaks who were building an imitation Ferrari 250 GT body on an old Ford V8 chassis and engine. We managed to get it around the block twice before we lost interest from lack of expertise and patience. My first car was a 1954 VW Beetle, but I traded 'up' to a 1948 MGTC and then on to a Triumph TR3. The Shandon drive-in cinema had opened in Elizabeth and became the centre of carnal pursuits for us young local 'wannabes'. I would keep a spanner under my seat in the TC and later in the TR3 to remove the steering wheel to provide more room for 'hanky panky' contortions.

Ah, the thrill of romance!

Chasing girls, racing cars and the burgeoning youth culture surrounding rock 'n' roll music were the unifying elements of young people of the time. My infatuation with rock 'n' roll music continued unabated, although I did listen to some modern jazz. My first records were 78 rpm discs such as Gene Vincent's 'Be-bop-a-lula' and, oddly enough, Stan Freberg's 'The Great Pretender', a parody of the Platters' hit. I was very much into 'humour' as a kid and always would be. Jerry Lee Lewis, Ray Charles, Chuck Berry and the greatest rock 'n' roll singer, Little Richard, filled my ears and my soul with their records. The Everly Brothers came next and songs like 'Bird Dog', 'Bye, Bye Love' and 'Wake Up Little Susie' seemed to fit right in with the arrival of my new pubic hair. I was becoming a teenager! Good golly, Miss Molly!

As a new suburb, Elizabeth North was still a work in progress in 1956 and only about fifty families had settled at that stage. Houses were at various stages of construction and became magnets for mischievous teenagers such as me. Minor instances of vandalism sometimes occurred but the half-built homes were ideal as ready-made hangouts and smoking dens. My parents did not smoke or drink but I found peer pressure too hard to resist and I began smoking when filter tips came into circulation. Viscount was my brand of choice, packets of five or ten were available. Smoking was even encouraged by doctors back then so who was I to argue?

Being a teenager was a cultural phenomenon that gave the younger generation a sense of identity separate from our parents. We were also surrounded by American influences and willingly welcomed them too. Entrepreneur Lee Gordon brought many of our music heroes to Australia, playing Adelaide's Centennial Hall. TV shows and movies were also highly influential: *77 Sunset Strip*, *Dragnet*, *Rawhide* and *Sgt. Bilko* were all popular on black and white TV while various rock 'n' roll movies all made their mark on us.

James Dean, Marlon Brando and Elvis were our 'Holy Trinity'. Motorcycles and leather jackets were appearing in suburban clubs, and gangs made up of guys named 'Nugget', 'Kicks' and 'Springy', began posturing around the streets of Elizabeth North although 'rumbles' were infrequent.

I hung out with other 'wannabes'. John Hough was my best mate; his family had a TV set and owned good records to listen to, while his older brother rode a Norton Dominator motorbike. They lived next door to the White family from Scotland, and we were besotted with the daughter, Joyce; an Ava Gardner type – lovely but aloof – and easily the best-looking girl around. She was out of my league but luckily, the girl who lived next door to me was always willing!

We would have 'record hops' in the newly built Community Hall at St Peter's Lutheran Church and we would all bring our favourite discs along to dance to. I found a great jiving partner named Pat and we were regarded as the best among our peers. One night in 1958, I arrived wearing my dad's cream sports jacket, which draped fashionably down below my knees, and around my neck was a cardboard guitar on a string that I had made. I did a pretty fair job of miming to Elvis' 'All Shook Up' but the record player broke down and I continued singing for real while busting out the moves. I received a nice round of applause from my buddies; a humble taste of things to come.

I was hooked.

Sitting in my 1948 MGTC, my first sports car, in front of our family home in Elizabeth East … 'the house that Harry built'. Note the lack of trees (which would come later) but I am still amazed at my father's architectural prowess.

******

My father Harry hatched a plan to build a family home for us, thereby freeing us from the rental of 51 Knighton Road. He bought a block of land on the slopes of the foothills of Elizabeth East and began designing a functional and economically viable house ... he was from Yorkshire after all! For the next eighteen months or so he filled every hour away from GMH constructing and erecting our home at 43 Northampton Crescent. Dad built it from the ground up using favours from friends and colleagues. I was a reluctant labourer and at age sixteen I was much more interested in being a teenager and all that went along with that.

Every building block was made by hand and when expert tradesmen were required to plumb or wire he would hire them and watch them closely. He would then fire them and carry on with what he'd learnt.

The house was of basic design with a flat roof and of little aesthetic appeal but included a couple of Harry's original ideas. The large picture windows opened and closed by sliding away into the wall cavities revealing adjoining fly screens, and most of the bedrooms were furnished with handmade furniture, again of spartan but practical design. We moved in as soon as the house became liveable – i.e. the windows and doors were in – and then Dad put the finishing touches on his proud project while we lived in it.

Although I assisted in my own lazy way, I was still in awe of my father's determination and skill in so many ways. I know he was sad to leave his achievement when the time eventually came, later on. I recently drove by number 43 and lingered outside what now looks to be a house so small and insignificant, but it remains a testament to Harry Shorrock, master homemaker!

CHAPTER 5

The Twilights

As the 1960s dawned, my high school days were coming to an end. I passed my leaving exam in year 10 and still hadn't decided my future, so I tried following Dad into fitting and turning at the Weapons Research Establishment (WRE) where he had worked. I only lasted a couple of months and, after spending most of my time filing down a block of steel, I quit days before signing on for a four-year apprenticeship.

I was fairly good at drawing so I applied for a couple of jobs as a commercial artist before being accepted as a junior draftsman in the SA Mines Department and began making my way in the world as a commuter into Adelaide, five days a week. I was also the lunch boy for the office but I enjoyed my time in map production. During my time there, we were all shocked by the assassination of President Kennedy in November 1963, the first of those 'where were you when' days that were to become increasingly frequent during the 1960s.

I worked alongside a guy named Peter Knoblauch, who was in a vocal quartet called the Four Tones which, along with the Penny Rockets, was one of Adelaide's first rock 'n' roll bands. I saw them perform at their regular Friday night gig at the Greek Club and was really impressed with their harmonies. One day, Peter informed me that one of the guys was leaving the group and, having heard me singing along as we worked, thought I was good enough to be his replacement.

Trying very hard to look like Steve Marriott from the Small Faces, even parting my hair down the middle. Sartorial elegance, circa 1965 … checks go with stripes in those days it seems.

I auditioned with the group and was accepted. Wow! I couldn't wait to tell my parents and my mates. I began practising with them and making plans in my head but imagine my shock when a few days later the guy who left decided to re-join. I tried not to show my disappointment but what a let-down.

I remember driving down the road in my VW and my mate Mike Sykes was coming along in the opposite direction in his Vee Dub. We both stopped in the middle of the road and wound our windows down to talk. The conversation was brief and went something like this:

Me: I've been sacked by the Four Tones.
Mike: Why don't we form out own group?
Me: Yeah ... good idea.

... and then we drove off.

Mike Sykes and Clem 'Paddy' McCartney were mates of mine who shared my interests in cars, girls and music. Like Mike, Paddy was a year older than me but he came from a similar immigrant 'two-hander' family (a boy and a girl) from Belfast in Northern Ireland. He drove a 1938 Buick Starlight 8, a real 'gangstermobile', that could fit a dozen people inside when we went to the local drive-in (with three in the boot!).

Mike was not so much into music, but we were members of a slot car club at the time were always singing along with our records. We asked a young Dutchman to sing bass but, unfortunately, he got into trouble with the law so we continued as a trio. We were called the Checkmates at the time, a typical doo-wop group of the early 1960s, but once we trimmed down to a trio I suggested the Twilights, after the changing colours of the Adelaide evening skyline.

It was 1962, and I was seventeen years old when we set off to who knows where. We didn't know what we were doing but that didn't matter. Nobody else did either. Luckily, the folk

boom was just taking off too, which made it very easy for vocal groups like us to expand our repertoire; they were very simple songs, with simple harmonies, as were most of the 'pop' songs of the day. In saying that, Peter, Paul And Mary introduced our generation to Bob Dylan, who was to become as big an influence on me as Elvis.

One of the first photographs of the Twilights, taken by Mike's father circa 1962. Mike has a nice curl going while my hair is too neat … I look like a young barber! And Paddy? Well, what can you say about that head of hair. Impressive.

We were enthusiastic rock fans who taught ourselves to become serviceable musicians. We soon found out that Mike had a strong falsetto, perfect for songs like 'Sherry' and 'Walk Like A Man' by the Four Seasons. We practised our rudimentary harmonic skills mainly in the Sykes family home and our songs of choice were fairly eclectic: 'Runaround Sue' by Dion and the Belmonts, 'Surfin' Safari' by Jan and Dean, 'At The Hop' by Danny and the Juniors, 'Blowin' In The Wind' by a young Bob Dylan and 'Tom Dooley' by the Kingston Trio.

Fame is a somewhat relative thing and our reputation began to spread to all parts of Elizabeth, and then beyond. Two venues in which we triumphed were St Peter's Mission Hall, run by the 'rogue reverend' Howell Witt, a bearded Welshman who certainly didn't look like your usual pastor, and the Matelot Club, which was run by Mike's parents in the Elizabeth South Scouts' Hall.

We knew of a Shadows-type band called the Vector Men, featuring brothers Frank and Alan Tarney on lead and bass guitar respectively, so we offered our services as a vocal group in return for theirs as a backing band.

Other bands journeyed up the Main North Road to challenge us: Trev and the Moccasins, Barrie McAskill and the Drifters, and John Perry and the Hurricanes, with whom we were to later combine when Frank and Alan disbanded to morph into John Broome and the Handels (I kid you not!). Often, two bands played at opposite ends of the spacious Salisbury Youth Centre on a Saturday night. It was a happening scene, as we teenagers were wont to say back then.

One night, we were treated to an interstate visit by the Gibb brothers, the young Bee Gees. Barry Gibb was about seventeen years old at the time, and twins Robin and Maurice just kids but, even then, they sang it like angels. They were already TV stars on *Bandstand* but I liked them immediately; Barry Gibb on guitar with the twins standing beside him harmonising. They were knockabout English migrants, like many of us, but they were also doing *Goons* jokes on stage and so I got them straight away. Barry would later write a song for the Twilights, for our first album in 1966.

Sometime in the early 1960s, I was shown a picture on the cover of Liverpool music magazine *NME* (*New Musical Express*) of four leather-jacketed young men who had been voted 'Liverpool's best band'. Their name was the Beatles but it didn't mean that much to me at the time until I had another 'Heartbreak Hotel'-type epiphany upon hearing 'Please, Please Me' in 1963. At first, it sounded to me like a new Everly Brothers song. Who were those guys?

When I saw the professionally-packaged, suited-up Beatles

With Adelaide DJ Bob Francis, the man who got the Beatles to add South Australia to their historic 1964 tour. The Twilights had just won a Beatles 'sound-alike' competition. I'm looking at the winning cheque as if to say, 'we won how much?'

with their long hair I had to reconcile that with the greaser-band image I saw on the front cover on that magazine from their days in Hamburg. They were exciting, and dangerous – and they sounded English, and not overtly American like other acts of the time like the Four Seasons, Bobby Vee and Johnny Tillotson!

So began the biggest single moment in the evolution of rock 'n' roll from dance craze to art form. We were besotted by the Beatles and everything changed! The group became the inspiration for writing and playing *original* material and John, Paul, George and Ringo led us all into a new era of creativity.

And thank God they did, because the music at the time was boring the shit out of everyone. The Beatles looked and spoke differently and with great humour and charisma, and they were totally anti pop star, and yet the irony is they became the biggest stars in the world.

By this time, I had left the Mines Department and accepted a

job as a junior civil design draughtsman with Salisbury Council. There I worked alongside an older guy named Patrick Boyle, who was to become a second mentor to me. Pat's interests in jazz and folk music, red wine, snooker and European cars rounded off my social education at the time. What else did I need?

Pat also sang in a trio called the Folk Three and after we became friends I became a lodger in his family home in trendy North Adelaide, my mum and dad having reluctantly agreed to me leaving the family nest. I had also met a vivacious, seventeen-year-old girl from Liverpool named Carol Birnie. She was gorgeous and quickly became my girlfriend. And she even spoke like a Beatle!

In early 1964, a 'Beatle Sound-alike' competition was announced in Adelaide and the three Twilights entered it and won with our version of 'Please, Mr Postman', the Beatles' cover of the 1961 Marvelettes song. We had taken to wearing black skivvies and had only just combed our hair forward, so much so

One of the first publicity photographs for the six-piece Twilights in 1965. (From left) Peter Brideoake, Clem 'Paddy' McCartney, me, Frank Barnard, Terry Britten and John Bywaters.

it was still curling up at the ends of our fringes. The Twilights were again backed by the Vector Men, who were peeved in not sharing the spoils, but we quickly realised that the times were indeed a-changing and we too would have to become an electric band at some point in the future.

At that time there were a lot of young bands emerging in Adelaide, such as Bobby Bright & the Beaumen, Johnny B Goode & Penny Rockets, Pat Aulton & the Clefs and the Hurricanes. Bitten by the British invasion bug, the Twilights had developed a solid bond with the Hurricanes. The chance arose to blend the two bands together and the Twilights became the six-piece outfit everyone came to know. Paddy and I joined forces with Terry Britten and Peter Brideoake on guitars, John Bywaters on bass and Frank Barnard on drums (two other Hurricanes members went on to other Adelaide bands – Kevin Peek to Johnny Broome & the Handels, and John Rupert Perry to the Vibrants).

Sadly, it came at a cost to Mike, my best mate, who was made redundant by the joining of the two bands. I had to break the news to him, that we were hooking up with members of the Hurricanes and going ahead without him – we didn't need three lead singers – but he was very gracious about it and agreed to step aside for the greater good.

That part of the business – sacking bandmates – was something I would never warm too. It would happen a lot over my career, especially with LRB, and eventually happened to me too. I'm still troubled by sacrificing Mike but he remains a friend and went on to rise to the rank of Wing Commander in the RAAF.

But these were early days, and I still didn't know where we were heading.

This was all in the lead-up to the Fab Four's visit to Australia in June 1964. Largely due to the efforts of local DJ Bob Francis, who gathered 80,000 signatures to convince Beatles manager Brian Epstein to add Adelaide to the tour itinerary, the Beatles played Centennial Hall on 12 June. And Adelaide exploded!

John, Paul, George and stand-in Jimmy Nicol (Ringo had tonsillitis and would not join the band until the Melbourne leg) were greeted by an estimated crowd of 350,000 people – most of them British immigrants – in the biggest thing to hit the city since the Royal tour. The Beatles were the *new* royalty and I took time off work with the Salisbury Council to line Anzac Parade, from the airport to the city, to welcome them. A group of us from the office stood part of a crowd that was four and five deep to catch a glimpse of the band and wave to them – a little bit of England coming

all the way to Adelaide – before going back to work and buzzing on that vibe for the rest of the day.

The Twilights did not attend the Beatles concert that night (the venue, Centennial Hall, had the worst acoustics in Australia and we had a rehearsal that night). Nor did we accept an invitation to attend the after-show party. Yes, there was a snob factor on our part: 'We're as good as them,' we said. 'They're nothing special,' we argued. Ah the arrogance of youth.

The Beatles came, conquered, and departed Adelaide, leaving us to carry on the legacy.

Our 'fame' was now Adelaide-wide and growing. The Oxford Club at the Goodwood Institute became our regular gig on Friday and Saturday nights with members paying 50 cents a ticket. We treated them to the best of British pop, with our 'note-perfect' covers of the hits of the day and 'dynamic' on-stage performances.

Self-managed and produced, we were encouraged by the success of Lennon and McCartney to write and record our own

Mastering my 'Beatle' look, copied from the black and white cover of the *With the Beatles* album … hair combed down on over the fringe and a black turtle neck sweater. I look more like a union official!

music. Terry Britten took to songwriting quite naturally while I, on the other hand, was content to enjoy the fruits of my labour and go after the girls.

We entered the charts in Adelaide in June 1965 with two original songs written by myself and the others. The A side was 'I Don't Know Where The Wind Will Blow Me' backed with 'I'll Be Where You Are' on EMI's Columbia imprint. The single got some airplay in Melbourne but, not surprisingly, failed to chart outside our hometown. Our second single, 'Come On Home', was a cover of a Hollies song and was released in October 1965 (the B side, 'Wanted To Sell' was written by Peter, Paddy and our drummer Frank Barnard).

'Come On Home' was picked up by Melbourne radio and came to the attention of club owner and budding band manager Garry Spry. One Saturday in Adelaide, we witnessed a guest appearance by 'Melbourne's answer to the Beatles' … the Flies! When they arrived, they could hear what they thought was a Beatles record being played over the PA and were stunned to see that is was us doing the song live. They were so intimidated by this they bombed that night. Spry quickly made us an offer to play at his Pinocchio's Disco in Melbourne.

We accepted the opportunity to play in Melbourne and took holidays from our day jobs (remember, we were still only weekend superstars) and set off for Melbourne for two weeks. We flew there and back on a TAA Viscount turbo prop airliner, a slight whiff of excess perhaps, but we felt we had the runs on the board and did not disappoint our new audience in 'groovy' Melbourne, which was a different world for us. These were professionally run clubs, not community halls run by volunteers, and they were frequented by hot chicks and guys in skivvies and corduroys driving Austin-Healeys.

Melbourne loved us and we knocked 'em dead – people were queuing around the corner to get in to see us. Such was our success, Garry Spry offered us a management deal and convinced

us to make Melbourne our new home. Back in Adelaide, we talked this over amongst ourselves and our loved ones and decided to quit our day jobs. All except our drummer.

Frank Barnard, our drummer, wasn't keen to make the over because he was married and had kids so we decided to approach Laurie Pryor, who had returned from London with the Handles, and he agreed to join us even if he thought we were a little too 'commercial'. He was a great drummer and became an integral part of our subsequent success.

I kissed Carol goodbye with every intention of her joining me later and drove out of my teenage years into adulthood, or so I thought.

We relocated to Lodge 52, Darling Street, South Yarra and became 'professional' musicians and entertainers. Melbourne was jumping in 1966 and the Twilights joined right in. We soon became *the* band to see and hear there and there were plenty of venues in and around the city to check us out: Sebastian's,

Paddy and Terry on stage with the Twilights. This photo reminds me of the night Terry was electrocuted on stage – he collapsed in a bundle and we continued on without him for an hour while he received ambulance treatment. Terry was arguably the best musician in the group, and easily the best songwriter as it would turn out.

Bertie's, Pinocchio's, Catcher, The Thumping Tum and Opus. I was twenty years old, I had a red sports car and I was a singer in a rock 'n' roll band. Yeah baby!

******

Many years later, I was the subject of a celebrity roast for charity at the hands of comedian HG Nelson, who has become a good mate. HG not only skewered me on the night, but the former Adelaide boy brilliantly put his own spin on my time in the Twilights:

The Twilights mushroomed out of Elizabeth in Adelaide's suburbs. The first time I clocked eyes on Glenn was in the Oxford Club in Pirie Street, Adelaide. Glenn was standing about onstage, waiting to chime in with a few oohs and maybe an aaah. What impressed me most were his pants. He was wearing the popular fashion of the time, a pair of flags. These were strides draped straight off the back of the buttock and falling into a 42-inch cuff that completely covered the shoes and a nice area of the feet. The slim-hipped buttocks were completely submerged in an ocean of yellow and orange-red tartan. It was pathetic. The pants were laughing at the hair. The kinky hair was trying to compete with the music for attention and the music was fighting to be heard over Shorrock's singing.

I followed the Twilights around. I could see them at the Octagon, the Princeton Club, the Castle Motel and the Scene. I bought their records. I would ring up radio stations and tell them to play the Twilights' new single. As you can see, there was bugger-all to do in Adelaide.

Thanks HG.

CHAPTER 6

The Happy Castle

In February 1966, the Twilights supported the Rolling Stones and the Searchers on their Australasian tour. Being hometown heroes, we were put on the Adelaide leg of the tour along with the Groop, with one Brian Cadd on piano. Many years later, I met Bill Wyman at a dinner party in France (as you do) and we had a great night, telling jokes and sharing stories. I asked him if he remembered us being on the bill that night but Wyman, the original bassist for the Stones and also the chronicler of the band's history said he did not, much to my disappointment. Well, we were pretty far down the list. For some reason all Bill could remember from that tour was New Zealander Ray Columbus and his hit 'She's A Mod'.

Inspired by the Small Faces we soon became a 'mod' band, resplendent in mod haircuts and the latest fashion of the day. We absorbed everything and were a great cover band. We became a very theatrical band who moved around the stage and engaged with the audience. A lot of it was me being me – a real show-off. Paddy would wear a gorilla suit or I would run across the stage in a Superman outfit with a pillow up my shirt. Anything to fire the crowd up.

We also played American soul – Otis Redding, the Four Tops, Marvin Gaye – and learned the latest Beatles records, *Rubber Soul* and *Revolver*, note for note. We met other bands that were to become both friends and rivals: the Groop, the Loved Ones,

Peter and me during the band's 'archaeological period' in the shadow of the Sphinx, Egypt. We stopped there on our way to England in 1966, fulfilling a long-held childhood dream to explore the ruins.

the Strangers and, of course, Adelaide bands that began arriving after our success. The Masters Apprentices, the Vibrants, Levi Smith's Clefs and James Taylor Move all made the trip over to Melbourne.

We signed with EMI and released our third single, 'If She Finds Out', nationally. Written by Terry and Peter, the song gained us fans in Sydney and Brisbane.

We had already released a rendition of Larry Williams' 'Bad Boy', which had been covered by the Beatles as a B side, but struck gold with the single, 'Needle In A Haystack' a cover of a Motown song originally cut by the Velvelettes in 1964. The song wasn't really indicative of what the band was doing live, but it was a fun song to perform and was a top-ten hit in most states, reaching the coveted number-one spot on the new *Go-Set* national chart in October 1966.

Commercialism was never far away from pop music in the 1960s. A giveaway of the era from Peters Ice Cream … a picture of your favourite band!

We began travelling across Australia regularly from Perth to Brisbane and employed our first 'roadie', Wayne de Gruchy, who would drive a VW Kombi with our gear and would pick up a hired PA system early in the evening and return that night or early morning. In those days we would do multiple 'spot shows' of twenty to thirty minutes duration in an average of three venues on the one night. Our fee for one spot was between $120 and $200, depending on the night. I recall once we were payed $600 to play the whole night – which was still only from 8 to 11 pm – but we were used to playing those hours back in Adelaide.

In one, twenty-four hour period we did four live spots and mimed our latest hit on a TV show called *Kommotion*. I particularly remember the *Kommotion* TV shoot for a number of reasons – it was filled up with most of the same crowd from Pinocchio's, and also for my encounter with actor Frank Thring. Sitting in the make-up chair before going on air, the imposing figure of Mr Thring, who I didn't know at all, leaned over to me and observed in his booming theatrical voice, 'And what have we here?'

'Ah,' I stammered, 'my name's Glenn and I'm from Adelaide. I'm a singer in a band.'

'A singer!' Thring bellowed. 'And what do you sing?'

I rattled off a few of our songs. Silence!

'And what do you do?' I asked finally.

'What!' he spluttered. 'What do I do?' And then he rattled off his credits: '*Ben Hur. King Of Kings. The Vikings!*'

'Oh, you're an actor,' I offered.

'Yes! I'm an *ac-tor!*'

I took notice of him after that because he was such an imposing figure; the first 'Shakespearean' person I'd ever met. Funnily enough, Frank and I would go on and do a movie together – if you could call it that (it was terrible) – called *At Last ... Bullamakanka: The Motion Picture* in the 1980s.

Although Frank Thring didn't know it, the Twilights

were now in the 'popstar echelon' in the fledgling Australian music scene. We weren't a teeny-bopper group like Zoot or the Valentines, although we did enjoy the attention of our fans. We were a tight band who sang harmonies well but weren't afraid to extend our boundaries and play Cream or Hendrix in later years. We were always at the top end of the *Go-Set* polls and various magazines' list of favourites, and our exposure on TV and radio was on the rise as the youth culture took hold of the country.

The Twilights did not have a lot of competition in Melbourne. There was the Groop, and the Loved Ones, but nothing much else. I remember seeing a teenage Joe Camilleri at several dances – he used to do a better Mick Jagger impersonation that Jagger himself – and he's still going strong today (so is Mick, by the way).

Sydney was more exciting at that time. The Easybeats and the Aztecs ruled there but new bands were quickly appearing. One such band featured an amazing young singer sporting a wild afro hairstyle named Doug Parkinson (in Focus), who took my breath away (and still does today). Billy Thorpe was a couple of years younger than me but was already hosting a live music show on Channel 7 and was quickly becoming a legend of the Australian music scene.

In Sydney we performed on a revolving stage at Sydney Stadium on Rushcutters Bay (where the Beatles played in 1964), alongside our closest rivals, the Easybeats. There were so many screaming girls (and boys) in the audience I recall being physically carried by security guys from the dressing room to the stage.

We recorded our self-titled debut album with house producer David Mackay at Studio 301 in Sydney in just a couple of days in mid-1966. The LP contained some specially-penned tunes from Barry Gibb and Hans Poulson, as well as covers representative of our live performances: the soul classic 'You Got Soul', which became our next single; a blistering version of the Yardbirds' 'I'm Not Talkin', the Who's 'La La La Lies'; the Moody Blues'

'Let Me Go' and the Hollies' 'Yes I Will', with some great harmonies by Paddy and me. We finished off with the Stones' '(I can't get no) Satisfaction', but then every band covered that song. The album was released in October 1966, by which time we were already on our way to England.

In July 1966, Hoadley's Battle of the Sounds was conducted for the second year. Originally started by *Everybody* magazine as a competition for unsigned bands, confectionery kings, Hoadley's, came on board and with the help of *Go-Set* magazine the contest really opened. We entered the finals with a certain amount of confidence, having already won the state title back in Adelaide.

The finals were held in Festival Hall Melbourne. Paddy had to step down to comply with the competition rules of no more than five members but we were still successful and he joined us for our victory 'lap'. I was the frontman and I was keen to sing the best parts. I didn't give him much room, I must say. Paddy had to compete with me for the best singing parts, which was hard for him, I know, and if I thought I could sing it better, I said so.

First prize consisted of $1000 prize money, full return passage to England on the Sitmar cruise line and a recording session with EMI London at Abbey Road! Subsequent competitions saw such acts as the Groop and the Masters Apprentices taking out first prize, until the competition ended in 1972.

By this time, my Adelaide girlfriend Carol had become a casualty of my falling in love with Sue Doran, a nurse from Prince Henry's Hospital in Melbourne, whom I had met at Pinocchio's. Carol, meanwhile, had seen the writing on the wall and had taken up with Idris Jones, an old friend and leader of the Gingerbread Men, so my guilt was somewhat assuaged.

Sue and I were a committed couple but she saw the opportunity opening for me in England and stayed behind in Australia when the group boarded the *Castel Felice* on 26 September 1966. We all bid an emotional goodbye to our respective wives and partners, which was especially hard for John Bywaters, as he left his lovely young wife and daughter behind, but as far as we were concerned the Twilights came first.

Although we were technically passengers, we offered to perform on the journey and the captain accepted so we played twice a week in the Verandah Lounge, on a stage made for a small trio led by a smelly accordion player. We enjoyed the experience and used our time to tighten up our show in time for our arrival in swinging London.

Beatle George Harrison had begun his love affair with all things Indian, so Terry especially wanted to get hold of a sitar when the ship docked in Colombo. We all piled into a rickety old taxi and instructed the driver to take us to the nearest dealer, who sold us a beautiful, but fragile, instrument that had to survive the rest of the journey. Terry spent long hours in our cabin trying to master his precious new acquisition, with about as much success as I had with growing hair on my upper lip. Terry would use his sitar to good effect on our later hits such as 'Cathy Come Home'.

We arrived in Suez at the entrance to the canal and Peter and I joined a tour of the famed pyramids and sphinx at Giza while the ship went through and met up with us again at Port Said. The great pyramid of Cheops was mind-blowing in its size. I have never since seen a structure of such immensity; the base was a quarter of a mile square and it reached 450 feet into the blazing blue sky. We followed our guide through tight stone passages until we reached the King's Chamber. There stood the sarcophagus that once contained the mummy of the pharaoh, now sitting empty and open in the dim torch light of the tomb, surrounded by thousands of tons of huge blocks of stone.

Out of curiosity, I hung back while our group left through the small opening in the corner, leaving me alone for a short while in the centre of the pyramid. I just wanted to see what it felt like and, whether or not I imagined it, I did feel an energy (or was it a just claustrophobia?). Needless to say, I didn't linger

The Twilights in the London winter of 1966–67. Note our warm Carnaby Street clobber and less than cheery dispositions. We were trying to be serious young insects!

for very long and soon caught up with the party, but that experience still resonates with me today, as it encouraged an interest in all things mystical and cosmic.

The *Castel Felice* was at the time the smallest ocean-going passenger liner at only 15,000 tons displacement, and was not equipped with the latest stabilisers, which resulted in the ship pitching and rolling for hours like a cork in a bowl. As the ship entered the Bay of Naples, we sailed into an eight-force gale, which caused us to hold anchor and ride out the storm until it was safe to dock alongside the port. Ropes were needed throughout the ship to keep passengers upright, but could not stem the flow of seasickness that seemed to come from everyone but me. I was to have my own health problem after docking.

Once we had docked that night we went ashore to recover and found ourselves in a nightclub with a live band. A crew member who was with us told the owner about us and we got up and did a few songs and got a good clap! I must have picked

Overleaf: A nicely composed publicity shot of the Twilights, back from London in 1967. Note the moustaches and beards from Terry and me … no longer just a pop band, and a little older and wiser for the experience.

up a 'wog' in Naples (boom boom) and by the time we reached Southampton my fever had risen to 108 degrees. As a result, I recall little of the arrival and journey up to London by train, other than our manager was not there to meet us at due to some problem back in Melbourne. We were met by EMI rep Roy Squires who put us all up for the first night in his flat in London. The Twilights thus spent our first night in London sleeping on the floor of Roy's flat.

We then moved into a basement flat in Nevern Square, Earl's Court, two of us in each bedroom, where we were to spend the next five months. Garry Spry

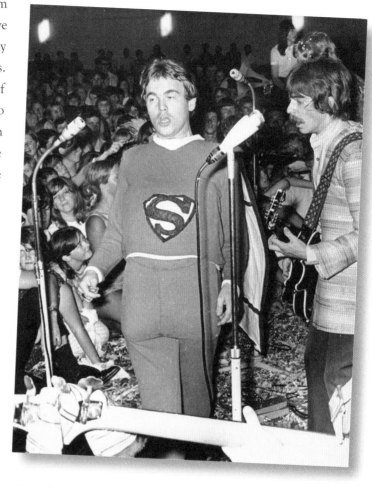

finally arrived a few days later and set about getting us some gigs. The Overseas Visitors Club was in Earl's Court Road, and most of its clientele and staff were Aussies so we were able to play there a couple of times. Our agent Nat Berlin (Irving Berlin's cousin), of the Lew Grade Organisation, however, had little success in getting us work and we spent a miserable winter in our digs in 'Kangaroo Valley' with next to no money for a decent Christmas lunch.

We did, however, have a booking to record at Abbey Road studios and we prepared ourselves with two original songs, '9:50', written by Terry Britten, and 'Young Girl', by our drummer

Laurie. The producer we would work with, Norman (Hurricane) Smith who had engineered of all the Beatles recordings up to *Rubber Soul* as well as producing Pink Floyd's debut album, had gotten hold of a Hollies song called 'What's Wrong With The Way I Live' and we would record that as well.

We showed up at the famous studios in the gloom of late afternoon on 6 January 1967. For the first time that year, a light snow was falling when as we arrived in two taxis, which also carried our gear. When we signed in at the front desk, the doorman informed us that we would be using Studio 1 because 'the group' were in Studio 2.

'Which group?' we enquired.

'The Beatles, of course,' he said in his thick cockney accent.

We looked at each other and started laughing in awe and trepidation. We tried our best to concentrate on the matter at hand but we couldn't ignore the fact of our heroes were in the studio just up the corridor from us.

While the first backing track was being recorded, I crept up to the control room door of Studio 2 and could hear Paul McCartney's unmistakable voice singing the words, 'Penny Lane is in my ears and in my eyes.' Little did we know this was the start of the *Sgt. Pepper* sessions. History in the making and we were there.

Super Droop on stage in 1967. Usually I wore a bald wig to show what Superman might look like as an old man but it's disappeared from sight here … the outfit was actually a pair of red winter pyjamas with a giant 'S' sown on them and a couple of pillows strategically placed in front.

We were too much in awe to try and make contact with the Beatles but famed producer George Martin came into our studio to listen to what we were doing and commented, very Prince Phillip-like, 'It's sounding good, carry on chaps.' At one stage, the other George (Harrison) walked by the open door of our studio carrying guitars and sitar. Thinking back to their Adelaide visit just three years before, the Beatles were now light years ahead of everyone else in the game, especially us. They were untouchable.

We recorded three songs that never to be forgotten night and left Abbey Road around midnight with stars in our eyes, literally! The tapes sounded good to us, and to EMI, and we released

'What's Wrong With The Way I Live' as our next single, with '9:50' as the B side. It was a top-ten hit in Australia but it struggled to get airplay in England, with local radio opting to play the Hollies' version. Lead singer Allan Clarke later graciously remarked that our version was much better than the one the Hollies did.

After our brush with what felt like success, we returned to twiddling our thumbs in our increasingly depressing flat in the 'Valley'. We spent our time waiting for letters to arrive from home as that first snowfall turned into a full-scale blizzard.

During this snowstorm I journeyed an hour by train to visit my mum's family in Kent. My cousin Geoffrey was preparing to move with his new wife Margaret into their first home in the coal-mining valleys of south Wales. I offered to help with the move to give me a change of scenery for a while and enjoy the warm hospitality of Margaret's family in their miners' cottage. Geoffrey and I slept side by side on the floor of the sitting room and during the night awoke to find ourselves safe in each other's arms. Floor sleeping was obviously popular at that time.

One of the few gigs Nat Berlin sent us on was to play the Cavern Club, the spiritual home of the Beatles, in Liverpool. This, of course, was exciting news for us. We drove ourselves up the M1 in a hired van and found our way to the front door where a sign stated, 'The Beatles played here 292 times!' It was historic stuff as far as we were concerned and we were thrilled to be a small part of it. Our reception from the locals was good enough to be asked to play again the following Sunday afternoon, if we wouldn't mind sleeping on the floor in the office upstairs, which we happily did. Back on the floor, boys!

We used a fencing club's change room across the lane to shower in the morning. During the afternoon, my watch and some of Terry's guitar accessories were stolen from the dressing room before we drove back to London that night. It was a bit of a downer but not too many can say they 'did the Cavern' … even if it was only twice.

The biggest shock to us in London was the high standard of so many groups who were not even known. It was hard for us to get jobs paying good money. By this time the long separation from our loved ones and our fans back home was taking its toll.

While in England, Sue and I wrote to each other and strengthened our relationship with letters back and forth. Although Terry and Peter, happily single, weren't fussed, it was particularly hard on Paddy and John, who were both married. We were all homesick.

Not even a spot on the *Top Of The Pops* TV Show could change our decision to return to Australia. Perhaps that was another mistake on our part but Christmas and new year's had been pretty gloomy for us, living in a basement flat with no heating and one bathroom shared between six guys.

We put it to a vote and decided to go home. Before we left England, however, we had one more raid on Carnaby Street so we could be on the cutting edge of pop fashion when we got home. Which we were!

CHAPTER 7

Once Upon A Twilight

B ack on board the 'Happy Castle' we went in February 1967, playing our way back to Australia. The *Castel Felice* was scheduled to stop in Adelaide so Paddy's wife, Patricia; John's wife, Val; and my girlfriend, Sue drove from Melbourne to meet us. Another storm, however, thwarted the ship from docking so we had to turn out to sea within eyesight of our loved ones and continued on to Melbourne. This disappointing event, which made the front page of the *Adelaide Advertiser* newspaper, meant the girls had to drive back to Melbourne where we happily reunited two days later.

The Twilights' return was enthusiastically welcomed by our fans and we were relieved to be back among our people again, despite a touch of regret at not having too much to show for our efforts in England. We did have three songs recorded, however, and they strengthened our live performances as we kept busy playing shows across the country. 'What's Wrong With The Way I Live' was a top-ten hit in Australia, ironically kept from the top spot by the Beatles' 'Penny Lane', which had been released as a double-A single (with 'Strawberry Fields Forever') in February.

The Easybeats were national favourites but we more than held our own. We were envious of their success as a recording group but we knew we had the wood on them in a live situation. When it came to musicianship, they relied more on Stevie Wright's wild

The Twilights in our final year as a band; we had run our race as a group and the inevitable break-up was looming. We're looking cheerful enough but the end was nigh.

energy and showmanship than good playing. Late in our run of six years together, the Twilights shared another revolving stage with Stevie and the boys on the reverse half of the stage of the Trocadero nightclub in Sydney – yet another venue that has sadly since disappeared.

Back in Melbourne, Sue and I decided we should marry and did so with her parents' blessing. We were married at the Uniting Church on Chapel Street in Windsor. Laurie Pryor was my best man, alongside John and Paddy as groomsmen. Terry and Peter decided to boycott the happy event because they didn't believe in marriage at that time!

My family came across from South Australia for the wedding, as did my friend Patrick Boyle and his wife Sarah. He managed to drink too much and helped himself to items of china and cutlery from the wedding reception which was held at the Menzies Hotel on Spencer Street. He later repeated this act of petty larceny at my second marriage by making off with Graeham Goble's jacket.

Sue and I set up home in Glenferrie Road, Malvern, across the road from former Prime Minister Robert Menzies. Although the marriage did not last, her mother Sally and I were to share a long-standing affection for each other in the ensuing years. I have been incredibly lucky with both of my mothers in law.

1967 also saw the release of the much-anticipated Beatles album, *Sgt. Pepper's Lonely Hearts Club Band*. The Suez Canal was closed due to the war between Egypt and Israel, which delayed the release here in Australia, but we had a friend named Richard Bence who would fly records in with Qantas, meaning we were able to hear them before anyone else and learn how to play their songs live a month before they got on the radio.

This wouldn't happen in these days of instant communication, of course, but it provided another Twilights 'legend' – we became known as the band to see if you wanted to know what the Beatles were up to. I still remember Richard, Terry and I listening in awe to *Sgt. Pepper's* on his stereo one magical night.

In November 1967, our new single 'Cathy Come Home' scored with the fans and was our last top-ten hit. We were also heavily influenced by other artists and we added Cream's 'Sunshine Of Your Love', Traffic's 'Dear Mr Fantasy' and Hendrix's 'Purple Haze' to our repertoire. Terry and Peter were composing material in the same vein and this would impact on our second album *Once Upon A Twilight* in 1968.

Another significant thing happened that year followed our support of a tour by the Who and Small Faces. Terry, John and Peter bought three, 100-watt Marshall amps from the promoters of the tour after they were deemed too expensive to ship back to England. Our on-stage 'fire power' was tripled and I didn't hear myself sing for the next two years.

We recorded 'Once Upon A Twilight' at Bill Armstrong's AAV (Armstrong Audio Video) studio in Albert Park with engineers Roger Savage and Ernie Rose, who were to remain close friends for the next couple of decades. Ernie and I work together occasionally to this day and AAV studio in South Melbourne was to become the centre of my recording life for many years after.

Our second album was released in June 1968 to mixed reviews; some thought it was a poor imitation of *Sgt. Pepper's* and it was certainly an ambitious project at that time for us. It even had a gatefold, die-cut, pop-up 3D cover depicting us as medieval knights in a fairytale landscape. Everyone was doing a concept album at the time so we thought we'd give it a crack!

Terry was writing songs in the psychedelic style; he'd taken LSD and had a personal 'epiphany'. We were singing through Leslie speakers and playing sitars because the Beatles had done it on *Sgt. Pepper's* and we wanted to try as many different techniques as possible. Singing through a microphone hidden under the strings of a piano trying to get a new sound ... hey, the Beatles had done it and sold millions! With the release of the album came our eleventh single, 'Always', which failed to go anywhere.

Our chart successes were beginning to dwindle although

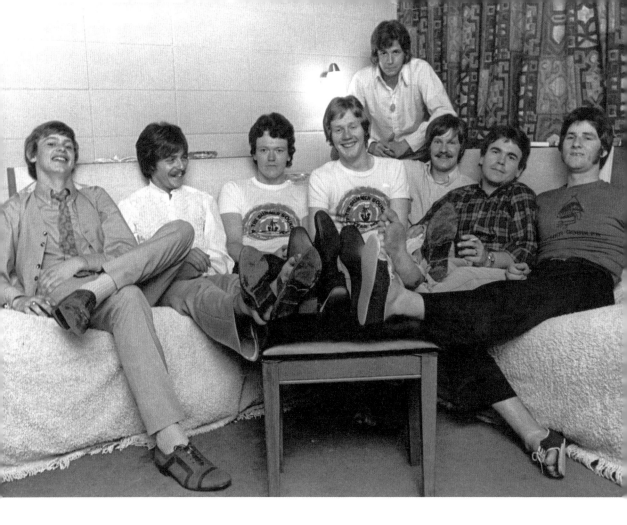

we still had a great live reputation and we even experimented with performing comedy. We would put on costumes and props and act out a farcical melodrama in between our 'sets' on stage. I played a clumsy parody of Superman, 'aged sixty-five', complete with bald wig (unnecessary now of course) and saggy leotard with a pillow shoved inside, who saves 'Teresa' Britten and child from the wicked landlord, played by John Bywaters. My character became known as 'Superdroop' and we persevered with this extra theatrical dimension, just to entertain ourselves, more than anything. Sometimes Paddy would do an entire show in a gorilla suit.

We were still doing good business and were in demand in Melbourne but it was proving difficult to maintain interstate interest. Surprisingly, a TV production company offered us a 'Monkeesesque' TV show of our own called, not surprisingly, *Once Upon A Twilight*. We filmed the pilot, which also starred a young Ronnie Burns and comedienne Mary Hardy, in Victoria and things looked promising for a while, but when the necessary sponsorship failed to materialise the project fell through.

We started to panic, I think. The previous year we had released the promotional record 'Bowling Brings Out The Swinger In You' (backed with 'Bowling Brings Out The Swinger In You' instrumental version) for EMI ... that was downright embarrassing. We released the double a side 'Tell Me Goodbye' and 'Comin' On Down' in August 1968, but it too failed to chart. Our next single 'Sand In The Sandwich' was pretty desperate stuff. This seemed to be the beginning of the end for us and we were running out of motivation and steam.

We decided to leave Garry Spry's management and EMI introduced us to Mick Conlin, an Irishman who had supposedly once been a tour manager for Cliff Richard. Mick became our manager but he was unable to stop the 'bleeding' at home and so suggested we return to the UK and give it another shot. Plans were begun for a departure but, suddenly, Laurie decided he didn't want to go overseas for a third time (he had first gone there with John Broom and the Handels) and returned to Adelaide to pursue a 'jazzier' path.

Paddy and John had misgivings too, both having young families, but when Terry's enthusiasm started to waver, I knew it was all over. We tried a couple of drummer replacements but none was as good as Laurie and we decided to call it quits in early 1969. The band had been together for six years and, in true Musketeer fashion, it was 'all for one and one for all' or nothing!

The Twilights played their last concert performance at Bertie's disco, Melbourne, in January 1969. The moment was bittersweet. The breakup of the Twilights was not something that we planned. It all happened over a couple of days. Our final single, '2000 Weeks', is pretty much a Terry Britten solo record. I don't think we even played on it.

John, Peter and Paddy decided to go back to Adelaide and I moped about in a state of shock, lost in my sadness at parting from my best mates who had been my 'brothers' since 1962. Terry decided to return to London and further his songwriting career and Mick Conlin went with him for the ride, saying that he had a lot of contacts in England.

I ended up going back to London with Axiom the following year but when Terry said he was going to London by himself, I bit my tongue when I should have spoken up and said that I'd come too. Perhaps I was waiting for him to ask.

Terry has developed a reputation as 'songwriter for hire' par excellence over the past five decades. He wrote 'Devil Woman' and 'Carrie' for Cliff Richard; the Grammy-winning 'What's Love Got To Do With It' (with Graham Lyle) and 'We Don't Need Another Hero' for Tina Turner, both monster hits, and his songs have been covered by everyone from Olivia Newton-John and Celine Dion to Michael Jackson and Lenny Kravitz. He opened a much sought-after recording studio in Richmond, installing some ex-Abbey Road equipment that had recorded the Beatles and sundry others, thereby anticipating the rediscovery of 'analogue' recording, so popular nowadays with young (and old) musicians. It has been one of my regrets that we haven't been able to work together over recent times but he did give me two lovely songs for my recent album, *Rise Again*.

Peter Brideoake turned his hand to classical composing and TV soundtrack work. Majoring in cello, he earned his teaching degree and taught music at Adelaide University.

Paddy McCartney and John Bywaters returned to Adelaide and resumed their working life and raised their families. John runs a business in Adelaide but still plays music. Paddy went

The Twilights performing at a 3XY concert held at a soccer ground on Punt Road in Melbourne, 1968. We are wearing our Indian-influenced garb which was all the rage back then. Terry is in bare feet (no OH&S then either) as John plays in front of a tall speaker box with the amplifier sitting precariously on top.

back to installing televisions for Canberra TV and is now a social worker in Adelaide. I recently caught up with them both on stage during the Adelaide Fringe Festival.

Laurie Pryor took up drumming duties with Chain and performed with the house band for the musical *Hair* in Sydney in the early 1970s. After undertaking various studio sessions and forming the early seventies prog-rock outfit Healing Force, Laurie fell into the drug scene and ended up back in Adelaide driving taxis. Things didn't work out too well for him and he later took his own life.

The Twilights have always been my favourite band and we still share a special bond today.

******

You may have noticed that I refer to the Beatles a lot. I cannot stress enough what the Beatles meant to my own musical journey and to countless others, and their influence is still as strong as ever to this day. Mind you, I'm easily influenced! I make no apologies for adding my voice to the throng of fans, forever growing with each generation, in saying they reached the summit of the mountain so many times during their career while the rest of us just made base camp.

But it's funny how the universe works, putting us at Abbey Road at a pivotal time in music history in 1967– which remains one of the greatest experiences of my life. I have often wondered what would have happened had we plucked up the courage to introduce ourselves to our heroes. We were too scared of being rejected: 'Sorry lads, far too busy,' but if they'd warmed to us who knows what could have happened?

I was petrified of meeting John Lennon because his reputation was that he could cut you to pieces with his wit. As a young man in Adelaide I had that dream, like most people of my generation, that they too could be a Beatle. When the phone rang, I would have the same daydream: is that John Lennon on the phone? 'Glenn Shorrock?' he would ask. 'Lennon here. We need a lead singer for the band. Can you get to London?'

After LRB released 'Reminiscing' in 1978, the song allegedly became a personal favourite of Lennon's (according to his former girlfriend May Pang). It's a lovely thought, if true, that John played our disc.

I try not to dwell too much on what would have happened if John Lennon had lived; it's still very much an unspeakable tragedy what happened to him. But I think they would have recorded again. Maybe even just Lennon and McCartney would have done something together, which would have been really interesting. But those sorts of hypotheticals do no-one any good. He's gone and we're all the lesser for it.

When I was first in London, the Twilights went to a couple

Performing 'Honey Don't' with Ringo Starr on *Parkinson* in 1982. Ringo dropped his sticks twice but no-one noticed. It was a real coup to be on Parky's show back then, and I managed to do it twice. Michael's a lovely, charming man.

of clubs hoping to rub shoulders with our heroes. I literally bumped into Paul McCartney at Blaises Discotheque in Queen's Gate one night. Thank god for Paul, who has both protected and promoted the Beatles legacy all these years, when all John wanted to do when he was alive was to destroy it. Paul has been the guy who has carried on the journey. God bless him!

Most Beatles fans fell into two groups – John's fans or Paul's fans – where I was probably a George fan in those early years. I immediately warmed to him, and his whole Indian music and mysticism thing. George's wife Patty introduced the Beatles to the Maharishi Mahesh Yogi and, having suffered the passing of manager Brian Epstein the same year as their biggest success, this caused much self-examination on their part.

I, like the rest of the world, followed these events with much interest. So, when the 'giggling guru' came to Melbourne in 1968 Terry Britten and I attended his lecture at Monash University, where we had performed regularly over the years as a band. We were subsequently initiated into the Transcendental Meditation

(TM) doctrine, after paying an entrance fee of approximately one week's wages and received our personal private mantras.

I had an open mind about it all and actually did experience a moment of bliss during meditation. It has been a part of my life for years now with lots of gaps along the way filled with that old black magic, hedonism. I have often been a 'fallen disciple' and I'm certainly no teacher!

In 1982, Michael Parkinson hosted a series of interview shows from Australia. Being well-known as a 'cricket tragic' – he is a Yorkshireman after all – it also just happened to coincide with our summer of cricket and Michael and I got on very well socially due to our love of the game. I was a guest on his show a couple of times, the first with Barry Humphries, another idol of mine. Parky invited Jo and I to lunch one day with another friend of his, the shy and retiring Billy Connolly.

It turned out to be the greatest lunch I have ever had. Billy was still drinking then and we had a riotous meal at Doyles on Watsons Bay in Sydney with 'lashings of ginger beer and some jolly japes'. We then repaired back to our home for more of the same. Billy and Michael never drew breath and told some wonderful stories. Jo and I woke the next morning with our stomachs aching from laughing.

Billy told his favourite football joke about the rivalry between Celtic and Rangers in Glasgow, his hometown, which goes into my book as the greatest story ever told; even better than Woody Allen's 'The Moose', and Billy told it to us live! Of course, Michael is no slouch at telling anecdotes either, having met and interviewed everyone you could possibly think of.

I made another appearance on the show promoting my single 'Rock 'n' Roll Soldier' in 1982 and this time Parky's special guest was Ringo Starr. I was asked perform my song with my band and then have Ringo sit in with us on drums as I sang his signature tune 'Honey Don't'. I was there in a heartbeat.

I noticed Ringo and wife Barbara Bach were both a bit 'merry' (I found out later a whole bottle of Courvoisier was consumed during taping). Ringo pulled it off with aplomb, despite dropping his sticks twice! Luckily my drummer Mark Kennedy covered nicely for him and I was thrilled to have performed live with a Beatle.

Sitting alongside the lovely Barbara Bach and her husband Ringo Starr on the 'Parky' show. Years later, when I met Ringo in Cannes, he told me he didn't remember being in Australia at all … or anything about the entire decade.

Years later, Jo and I found ourselves checking in alongside the Starrs at Cannes Airport. Jo urged me to make contact again and so I reminded a somewhat puzzled Ringo about our last meeting, to which he responded, 'I don't remember Australia and I don't even remember that decade.'

He was, of course, his famously charming self, now sober.

The Axiom

CHAPTER 8

Axiom

My mood following the demise of the Twilights was tempered by Garry Spry, who offered me a stint as an agent in his newly formed Australian Management and Booking Organisation (AMBO), alongside Jeff Joseph, Peter McKenna (The Loved Ones) and Bill Joseph (The Vibrants). One of the bands I got work for were the 'Brisbane' Avengers, a teen-pop outfit so called by people in the industry because there were also the New Zealand Avengers playing gigs at the same time. My involvement in AMBO evolved into me becoming the Avengers' manager for a time.

I quite enjoyed being part of their lives but truth be told, I didn't like staying in the wings when they went on stage. I got the itch for performing again.

At that time, Ian 'Molly' Meldrum hosted many a party for us 'creative types' at his home in Melbourne. One Saturday night I got talking with Brian Cadd whose band the Groop had also recently broken up. Brian, along with Don Mudie, had written some very good songs in that band – 'Woman You're Breaking Me' and 'Such A Lovey Way' to name but two – and, over some alcohol, we discussed getting a new band together.

Suffice to say, Brian and I forged a friendship that survives to this day. I wasn't particularly close to him at the time – that would come much later – but we were both bitten by the new country rock genre coming out of the US, particularly from

A *Go-Set* foldout poster from the period of Axiom: (from left) Don Mudie, Don Lebler, Brian Cadd, me and Chris Stockley. This poster was hung on the walls of bedrooms all over Australia, by the look on Cadd's face he is obviously up to no good.

the Band after their seminal 1968 album *Music From Big Pink*. We both thought it was an exciting way for rock 'n' roll to go. The Beatles were breaking up and it was as if the musical baton was being passed back to America.

That meeting with Brian led to the forming of Axiom. Don Mudie quickly came on board on bass and we pilfered guitarist Chris Stockley from country-rock outfit Com-Pact and drummer Doug Lavery from Perth heartthrobs the Valentines. Former Twilights roadie Wayne De Gruchy managed us and we hired a giant roadie called 'Lurch' who could lift a Hammond B3 organ by himself. Sometimes, he also lifted Brian on and off the stage.

We were given the embarrassing title of 'supergroup' by the Australian music media, a name coined overseas to describe such bands as Blind Faith and Crosby, Stills, Nash and Young. Any publicity is good publicity but it actually was a millstone around our necks.

We began rehearsing a repertoire in the Nathalia Football Club, in central Victoria, near Don Mudie's family home. This time I refused to sleep on a floor and made Chris Stockley do it. We rehearsed long into the winter nights in the freezing cold clubhouse, warmed by cheap scotch 'tea', and began to grow our hair and beards to go with a new-found authenticity. Axiom embarked on a lurching tour of Victoria and began to gain some traction.

Brian and Don had penned a song called 'Arkansas Grass' about the American Civil War (shades of the Band, I know) and we put it out as our first single in August 1969 on EMI subsidiary Parlophone, the Beatles' original label. We even filmed a

The 'Caddmobile' in front of the Axiom headquarters in West Dulwich, London in the early 1970s.

promotional clip for the song – and this was years before music video and MTV – wearing Civil War–era clothes and stumbling across the Victorian countryside. It became an instant hit and reached the top-ten on the Australian charts.

'Arkansas Grass' attracted some criticism in its day; many thought it was about marijuana (a situation not helped by the film clip showing us passing a smoke around) but it was really an anti-war song at the height of the Vietnam War. It was a protest song, but it was criticised for being 'too American' in tone.

Doug Lavery only lasted a couple of months before following his American girlfriend back to the US, where he stayed for forty years (our paths would cross again in the future). I had bonded with Don Lebler, a lanky drummer from the 'Brisbane' Avengers, and he was enlisted to take Doug's place.

Axiom adopted a suitably serious image for the time but we soon relaxed on stage after partaking in more drinks. On stage, I was often holding Chris upright with one hand and stopping Brian from falling off his stool with the other! One night in a club on the Gold Coast, the cast of *Hogan's Heroes* (on a promotional tour) were on a table in front of Stockley who, as well as being drunk, was also vision impaired ... blind drunk! Chris managed to fall off the stage onto the celebrity table not once but twice. *Stockley!*

Life for me revolved around the band and the accompanying partying. My wife Sue and I had moved into a flat nearer to her mother Sally. The Dorans were going through rough times; Sue's father was by now an alcoholic and becoming increasingly violent (he once threatened me with a cricket bat) and her brother had fallen in with local 'crims' and was doing time in Bendigo Gaol. We visited him often.

We recorded our first album, *Fool's Gold* in early 1970 at Armstrong's newly-installed eight-track recording studio in Melbourne. Unusual for the time, the thirteen tracks were produced by the band. All the songs were written by Brian and

Don and were full of Australian references with a country-rock influence: 'Mansfield Hotel', 'Ford's Bridge' and 'Once A Month Country Race Day'. I know Brian was really upset when he was asked to tone down the Americanisms in 'Ford's Bridge', which was originally called 'We Can Reach Georgia By Morning'. He just didn't understand why he had to change the words.

The ballad 'A Little Ray Of Sunshine', inspired by the birth of the daughter of a couple Brian and Don knew, was released as our next single in March. 'A Little Ray ...' was another top-ten hit and became an Australian classic that I'm still singing to this day. To be honest, I never liked my vocal on that record because I thought I sang a little flat in a couple of places, which is why I have re-recorded it a couple of times over the years.

Many people thought it was about Brian's kids, but the beauty of the song now is that it's about everyone's kids. If I had a dollar for every time someone has come up to me over the years and said, 'You know what? We played that song ...'

'... when your daughter was born?' I finish.

Now I perform it for the granddaughters of fans. I'm chuffed to sing it, but it's really a compliment to Brian and Don for writing such a great song. Sadly, their relationship fell out over money in more recent times and they haven't reconciled.

Axiom was only a little over a year old and already we were thinking of having a crack at England again. As with me, Don and Brian had first experienced England with the Groop after winning Hoadley's Battle of the Bands (in 1967). I was very keen to go again. Our manager Wayne made a deal with Sitmar Cruises for Axiom to play our way back to London on, none other than, the *Castel Felice*. It was as if the Happy Castle was haunting me. We even stooped to advertising the Sitmar line on the cover of

The cover of our album *Fool's Gold* taken on the deck of the *Castel Felice* to promote our voyage to London in 1970. Ok, so it's no *Sgt Pepper's* but we 'sold our souls to the devil' so to speak to secure free passage for us and our partners.

our album *Fool's Gold*, featuring all five of us grinning around the ship's steering wheel wearing sailor's hats. No shame in that; it did facilitate free passage for our wives and girlfriends.

This time we headed east across the Pacific and through the islands of Tahiti on through the Panama Canal, Curaçao on the north coast of South America, across the Atlantic to Lisbon and onto 'Blighty'. We played in the bar on the stern of the ship with our backs literally against the back railing. Don suffered from sea sickness and was often playing bass 'runs' while heaving over the side of the rail, while our audience and amplifiers slid across the deck.

What shall we do with the drunken sailors? Lock them up, of course! Peter Curtin, a mad friend of Chris Stockley's who was attached to our entourage, was forever being locked in the brig by the Master at Arms (our nemesis) for such behaviour. Pernod was still dirt cheap and of similar quality.

The *Castel Felice* called into Panama City prior to joining the convoy through the impressive canal and sailing into the Atlantic Ocean. Going ashore that night, we solicited a taxi driver to find us some 'weed' – not a particularly smart thing to do in Central America in 1970. We did score a bag of grass but on examination once back on board, it was quickly discovered that it was indeed grass ... from someone's lawn! Peter Curtin actually smoked it.

On arrival in London, we rented a large house in West Dulwich in London's south. Wayne de Gruchy was a good manager in that respect, and his forward planning paid off for us. Sue and I made a 'nest' for ourselves on the first floor, comprising of a bedroom and a bathroom, with a shared living room and kitchen on the ground floor. The front parlour became our rehearsal room and extra bedroom. There were ten of us living together, so compromises had to be made, especially in the bathroom and kitchen situation, but we seemed to get on pretty well with each other.

Somebody told Wayne that he could restore his thinning hair

by using raw eggs on his scalp and he was caught pinching our breakfast eggs from the fridge one morning and cracking them on his balding head!

Sue got a job as a sales assistant in a Kings Road boutique and I relied on her a lot because she had a regular job. I began writing songs and whiled away the time building model cars. I made contact with Terry Britten, who was working closely with old Adelaide colleagues Alan Tarney, Trevor Spencer and Kevin Peak, members of the old James Taylor Move band. They called themselves Quartet and were producing some great semi-acoustic music that I liked a lot.

Wayne had a publishing deal from Leeds Music and reported offers from Apple and Decca, but Warner Brothers showed the most interest and we prepared a showcase gig to show them what we could do. We invested in an old Bedford van, which was permanently parked outside our house in South Croxted Road and readied ourselves for our first gig. We raised a few eyebrows by playing Don Gibson's 'Sea Of Heartbreak' as our opening song but Warners were suitably impressed to sign us to a three-year contract.

The other significant event that happened at this gig was being introduced to stage monitors for my vocals for the first time. We thought they were leftover boxes from the PA system; 'What are they for?' we asked. But the monitors facing back at us on the stage allowed me for the first time to hear my voice above the guitars and drums. Over the years, I had trained my ears to hear the ambient sounds of my vocals from the PA speakers on either side of the stage and it was good to be able to hear my voice so clearly. I felt I immediately improved as a singer because I no longer had to shout to hear myself above the band.

We went into the studio with legendary American-born producer Shel Talmy, whose musical CV included producing hits for the Kinks, the Who, Manfred Mann and the Easybeats. Our single 'Father Confessor' was released in July 1970, but after

Another *Go-Set* poster of Axiom. We had three top-ten hits in three consecutive years in 1969–71 but we just didn't get our timing right … as Brian said, 'we zigged when we should have zagged'. Chris Stockley (far right) is obviously trying to hold up his pants!

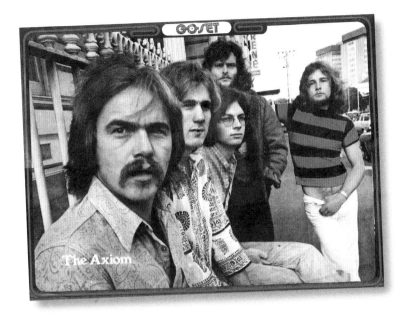

The Axiom

the success of our first two singles this one failed to chart at all in Australia, probably because we weren't there to promote it – I wasn't aware it was released at all!

We made some good progress as a band but it slowly dawned on us that England was not the place to be as far as our music was concerned. The UK had been forever altered by the break-up of the Beatles and was embracing glam rock. Bowie, Bolan, Slade and Sweet were de rigueur and our country-rock style was not as popular in England. As Brian Cadd famously remarked at the time, 'We zigged when we should have zagged.' Axiom should have gone to America, as Little River Band later proved, where our music would have been better accepted.

In London, I was being drawn more and more into the alternative lifestyle of meditation, macrobiotics and mysticism. I joined a group of ex-pats who met every fortnight in a cafe in Battersea for spiritual sessions led by a man named 'John Pilgrim' who professed to be in touch with the 'other side' as a medium. Brown rice and vegetables garnished with seaweed became my diet for a while, but Sue was living the good life with newfound friends on trendy Kings Road and our lives slowly began to drift apart.

We started work on our second album, *If Only* at the end of 1970 at Olympic Studios in London. 'My Baby's Gone' was the single released in Australia and this time, we flew home for a short tour to promote it. It was to become our third top-ten hit in three consecutive years. By then, I was pretty unrecognisable as the fresh-faced kid at the front of the Twilights – I was developing my radical 'Fidel Castro' look with beard and long, flowing hair. But we were confident our new album would be a success back home and break us in England.

While we were away, however, Shel Talmy added strings and horns to our songs and we were totally disappointed with the mix of the album when it was released. We made our displeasure clear to the record company, who did little to promote it or the single in England.

If Only was released in March 1971, by which time Axiom had ceased to be as a band.

As winter approached, Don Mudie developed a persistent lung infection and decided to return home to Oz. The Mixtures were also giving up trying to build on their hit 'The Pushbike Song' in England and Mudie, Stockley and Lebler joined up with a couple of their members and secured another 'play for passage' with Sitmar for the trip home. Two other members of the Mixtures, Idris Jones (now married to my old flame Carol Birnie), and Mick Flinn, stayed behind in England.

Don Lebler took over as the drummer with the Mixtures

but the band never repeated their early chart success. Chris Stockley went on to a very distinguished career in the 1970s with country-rock band the Dingoes. Brian Cadd returned home to Australia and had a string of hits with 'Show Me The Way' (with Don), 'Ginger Man' and 'Don't You Know It's Magic' (for John Farnham) in 1972, writing the theme song to the movie *Alvin Purple* in 1973 and working with Ron Tudor to form early indie label, Bootleg.

Me? I didn't want to go home having failed again so Sue and I stayed in England and moved into two rooms on the top floor of a Battersea terrace owned by my cousin Geoff (he let us have it for five pounds a week ... or was that a month?) We shared a bathroom with the downstairs tenants and cooked our meals on a two-burner range on the landing at the top of the stairs. Needless to say, Sue was not impressed by these conditions and she left me within a couple of months, our marriage over.

Sue wanted to continue on as a single woman living in London. We hadn't been doing much as a couple. Sue had her friends in the fashion industry and was partying hard while I was exploring music, mysticism and meditation – not really a great mix.

I was shocked, more so my ego, but after the anger and, yes, depression, dissipated I put it down to another lesson learned. By 1972, I was living alone in London with a small piano, a tape recorder, a black cat and a mood to match.

One day I was walking through Piccadilly when I rushed around the corner and collided somewhat painfully, head on, with Rolling Stone Keith Richards. Keith looked like death warmed over, even then, but he merely grinned at me and went on his way.

I didn't have the opportunity, nor the heart, to remind him that I had once been in a band that had shared the bill with the Stones on their 1966 Australasian Tour.

CHAPTER 9

Solo Esperanto

It was the early 1970s, and I had a few contacts in London, musical colleagues, friends and relatives, who helped keep my spirits up. I lived on brown rice throughout the week and hoped for an invitation to a weekend party to Bee Gee Maurice Gibbs' mansion in Hampstead, North London, where he lived with his singer wife Lulu. At least I knew I could eat and drink all I wanted, catch up with friends and then catch the bus home at dawn. Ah, the pop-star life!

I was writing songs, including an early version of 'Statue Of Liberty' which I made a demo of with the guys in Quartet. I had seen the movie *Planet Of The Apes* with Charlton Heston and that wonderful final image of the Statue of Liberty; I came out of the cinema with the idea for a song and wrote the lines:

Statue of Liberty,
Standing in the harbour,
This is America,
We try a little harder.

A favourite photograph of mine from a shoot I did with Geoff Hales in Kew Gardens in the rain. We used the resulting images for publicity purposes. (Courtesy Geoff Hales)

I couldn't remember the quote at the bottom of the statue so I just paraphrased, 'Give me your hungry, give me your tired, give me your homeless, give me your wanderers,' etcetera. The song would be recorded a couple of times in the coming years.

I managed to get a publishing deal with MAM Records, which

was owned by Gordon Mills, the manager of Tom Jones, Engelbert Humperdinck and Gilbert O'Sullivan. I was given an advance on royalties of around 1500 pounds so I asked if I could be paid at thirty pounds a week so it could keep me going for the next year.

I was hanging out with Geoff Hales, a friend from the Thumping Tum days back in Melbourne. He and his model girlfriend Gael McKay were living on a houseboat moored on the Thames near the Chelsea Bridge. Geoff was dabbling in photography, art and percussion and Gael was getting good work as a photographic model on the catwalks of London. One weekend, Geoff and I accompanied her to Paris on an assignment. I had purchased a little orange Fiat 600 in reasonable condition and we drove from London to Dover, before being ferried across to Calais then on to Paris. There, Gael introduced me to a Swedish model and we hit it off immediately, so to speak. It was

My 'bothy' in West Sussex was my hideaway for a year after the break-up of my first marriage.

a romantic adventure that I later wrote about in 'Seine City', one of my better songs I think. When I tell the story in concert that the song was inspired by a romantic weekend with a Swedish model, I add the punchline, 'His name was Björn' (cue laughter).

The three of us also enjoyed an 'alternative' week in Dumfriesshire in the south-west of Scotland in a quaint little cottage where we spent some glorious summer days rambling and eating brown rice and vegetables. Gael is still part of my life and a few years later she was instrumental in changing it for the better.

I recorded a couple of singles for MAM, the first being 'Purple Umbrella', which I sang in a broad French accent under the alias of Andre Escargot and Society Syncopators (actually Quartet as the backing band) in August 1971. Novelty songs were very popular in the UK at the time ... this one wasn't. Other songs, 'Let's Get The Band Together' in 1971 and 'Rock And Roll Lullaby' in 1972, were under my own name but fared no better. I also had 'No Full Moon' recorded – the song I had written for my 'girl next door' back in my home town of Elizabeth – by a B-grade English singer named Leapy Lee, whose career was well and truly over by then.

I was also scoring vocal sessions through my connections with the Aussie music 'mafia' in London at that time. My old Twilights producer David Mackay had set up a production house and Peter Gormley, an Australian entrepreneur I had never met before, was managing Cliff Richard and Olivia Newton-John at the time. Another Australian, ex-Strangers guitarist John Farrar, had briefly joined the Shadows and was also working with Cliff and Olivia. I was secretly hoping Quartet would ask me to be their lead singer; it was typical of me not to say anything directly to them and just hope that it would happen.

I met another nurse, a sweet girl named Irene, who helped me through those frustrating times. After moving out of my garret in Battersea I rented a 'bothy' in the West Sussex country village of Plaistow. A bothy is an outbuilding on a country house, and this one belonged to a Harley Street doctor who used it on weekends.

My tiny cottage consisted of two rooms, one up and one down, with a tiny bathroom, but it was in charming surroundings and quite peaceful – just me and my guitar and Rastus the cat. Irene would also spend her days off with me in this truly romantic setting. I used British Rail to travel to and from London but I needed wheels to get to my bothy from the local station, a few miles away. I bought a cheap scooter and a crash helmet and was soon weaving my merry way through the Sussex byways with just the occasional minor accident. I would also visit Russell Morris, newly arrived in the UK and within Vespa range, in the nearby hamlet of Liphook.

One day in 1973, I had a call from David Mackay; he had a musical project on the go, a 'rock orchestra', as he described it, and asked if I would be interested in coming on board. The group was centred around a string quartet out of Belgium – Raymond Vincent (violin), Godfrey Salon (violin), Tony Harris (viola), and Timothy Kraemer (cello). Italian brothers Tony and Gino Malisan were on drums and bass with three female backup singers in tow – Janice Slater from Australia, Joy Yates from New Zealand and Brigitte Dudoit from Hawaii – who had been Cliff Richard's backup singers. Bruno Libert on keyboards and Brian Holloway on guitar rounded out the band to an even dozen.

The band was to be called the Esperanto Rock Orchestra, a nod to the international language Esperanto and a fitting name for a group of made up of a dozen people of various nationalities. The

whole enterprise sounded intriguing, a fusion of classical music and rock, so I said yes. It wasn't as if I had anything else to do.

David Mackay rented country estate Clearwell Castle in Devon, in the west of England, for a month of rehearsals. It was rather grand but we managed to prepare some new material. I got my song 'Statue Of Liberty' included in our repertoire but the driving force musically was Raymond Vincent, a former first violinist with the Belgium Symphony. A virtuoso visionary on violin, Raymond was charismatic and, with Bruno Libert, wrote wild, avant-garde opuses in strange time signatures; very progressive and challenging to play and sing.

After another month of rehearsals at a farm in Belgium, David booked the group into Morgan Studios in Willesden, outside London, to record our first album. Armed with a couple of early songs, 'Black Widow' and 'Publicity', which didn't eventually appear on the album, David went in search of a recording deal. Polydor passed on signing the band (they had their hands full with Slade) but Los Angeles-based A&M Records were opening an office in London and rep Derek Green showed great interest in us.

David Mackay went to Los Angeles to meet A&M co-founders Jerry Moss and Herb Alpert, the latter of Tijuana Brass fame, and secured the band a three-record deal with a separate producer contract for him. We finished recording in TCR Studio in London with Ken Scott producing; unbeknown to us A&M London had taken the masters off David and given them to Scott, who would later have great success with Supertramp.

I didn't realise until years later that I inadvertently tipped off David that he had been replaced. 'Are you coming to the mix tonight?' David recalls me asking him when he rang.

'What mix?' David replied.

David had been cut out of the band that he formed by the record company. Obviously, I didn't take too much notice of the behind the scenes music politics.

More images from the Kew Gardens sessions with Geoff. (Courtesy Geoff Hales)

Esperanto went on a tour in Europe with UK folk-rock outfit the Strawbs and then toured the Midlands and North of England with 1950s-inspred US showband Sha Na Na (who were also signed to A&M). What a juxtaposition of musical tastes! We played gigs at the Roundhouse, the Shaw Theatre, the Rainbow, the Queen Elizabeth Hall in London, but also smaller venues in Newcastle, Manchester and Liverpool.

There is vision of Esperanto on YouTube playing a concert at the Bataclan Theatre, later the scene of a sickening massacre in 2015, in support of our debut album *Esperanto Rock Orchestra* in September 1973. I am wearing an open-vested shirt and hippy beads of the era, with my pop face on. There is some virtuoso playing from the string quartet but trying to fit all those voices into that musical format was crazy. The songs were incredibly complicated and it took me a lot of time and effort to get my head around them.

We lived as communal hippies, sharing dope, drink, clothing, macrobiotic food and other 'fringe benefits' of communal living (well, it was the 1970s!). But it wasn't reality. You can't live on brown rice and free love forever.

The Esperanto group photo on the gatefold of our first album … spot the lead singer (I'm in there somewhere).

110

As a twelve-piece band, the economics were not the best either. In fact, they were most prohibitive. Our tours were expensive to mount and we never got any feedback from the record company about how our album was selling.

Back in England, we met up again in a castle in Wales and started to prepare for our next album. The Welsh castle was supposedly haunted; I had my own room and lay awake nervously expecting a visit from 'the other side' (or Janice!), but sadly neither materialised. After several weeks of rehearsals, the group recorded some new songs which the record company promptly rejected.

So, Plan B was put in action. King Crimson producer and co-founder Peter Sinfield was brought in and our three soul sisters were let go. I was moved to co-producer of our second album and would also write some new songs and contribute lyrics when required. The band's new direction concentrated on the string quartet rather than the vocals, and Keith Christmas, a towering hippy straight out of a Tolkien novel, was brought in as the new frontman.

Esperanto's second album, *Dance Macabre* was released in 1974 and went even further 'out there'. At the time, the Electric Light Orchestra was breaking and their more commercial approach completely eclipsed the complexity of Esperanto. Jeff Lynne's ELO had stolen our 'rock orchestra' thunder. They recorded simple songs based on Chuck Berry chords, added strings and nailed it. I left Esperanto soon after.

Our 'rock orchestra' experiment was over, so I returned to my own language and recorded a single 'Daydream Sunday' that went straight down the middle of the road to nowhere! I moved back to London with Irene into a first-floor flat in Tulse Hill, close to Brixton. My sister Lynda moved into the ground floor flat with her boyfriend Chris Dawes, a young guitarist from Adelaide, on an extended working holiday.

I did anything and everything to eke out a living in London.

One weekend, I got a job up in Luton moving amplifiers for a heavy metal band. I can't recall the name of the band but it was a hard way to earn three quid!

I then got a call from Cliff Richard's office asking if I would like to join his backing group, which included Terry Britten, Alan Tarney and Trevor Spencer (three members of Quartet), as a singer for a four-week season at the London Palladium. The lads had recommended me to Cliff and the pay was about 100 pounds a week. I thought it over for a nanosecond and said yes. Irene and I went out to dinner that night to celebrate. It could not have come at a better time; things were starting to wear a bit thin.

I had my first taste of the big time, albeit in a supporting role, at the iconic London Palladium in Piccadilly, complete with dressing room and a stage doorman who called me Mr Shorrock! The opening night went well in front of a full house of Cliff's loyal fans. At the after party, manager Peter Gormley congratulated me on my enthusiastic performance before adding, 'But Glenn it's *Cliff's* show!' I was just trying to entertain the audience but was obviously overdoing it a tad.

I soon settled down and enjoyed eight shows a week in a truly professional show. Cliff is a terrific headliner and it was great to work alongside guys I'd grown up with in Adelaide a decade before.

But soon the bright lights dimmed and another long English winter approached. One morning, my old friend Idris Jones called me in obvious distress. His wife, our darling Carol, had died suddenly of an aneurysm at the age of twenty-three. He was shattered and I rushed to his side to do what I could to help him through the tragedy. She was the most beautiful, vivacious girl ever to come into our lives and was such a loss to so many. We had struggled to make our way into the music scene in England and this tragic event left us wondering about our priorities.

Again, the wheel would turn a few months later.

I had known Glenn Wheatley as the bass player of the Masters

Apprentices back in Melbourne in the 1960s but he had recently been involved with entrepreneur David Joseph in managing the New Seekers. In England with his wife Allison, Glenn had met members of the Australian band Mississippi, who had travelled there on the *Fairstar* and promptly broken up. Three key members, Beeb Birtles, Graeham Goble and Derek Pellicci, wanted to continue with a new line-up and Glenn wanted a to manage a band that he thought could break into America. But Mississippi needed a frontman, someone to sell their songs to the audience, and Glenn recommended me. Would I be interested in meeting with them with the view to becoming the lead singer in their new venture?

I didn't know much about Mississippi, although I knew of Beeb from his days in Zoot. Mississippi had a hit with 'Kings Of The World' in 1972, an acoustic song with wonderful harmonies in the Crosby, Stills and Nash mould, and had followed up with 'Early Morning'. Someone actually sent me a copy of Beeb's song 'Will I?' which Mississippi released in 1973, and I liked the harmonies I heard but didn't give it too much thought. In fact, living in England, I had missed out on a lot of Australian music in the early 1970s – the Daddy Cool phenomena, Sunbury '72, and the whole Billy Thorpe and the Aztecs revival.

I met with Beeb, Graeham, Derek and Glenn in London and we had a good discussion and sang some songs together. Graeham was from my hometown of Adelaide and Derek was a ten-pound Pom (albeit a decade after me) but I had not met either of them before. I was struck by how easy it was to blend with their voices and the songs sounded very promising, one of which was 'It's A Long Way There', which I really liked. We determined that if we were going to perform together on stage then the harmonies had to be strong and strident, rather than soft and pretty. As soon as we sang that opening line, 'Hey everybody ...' we knew we had something special.

We all agreed that England at the time was not where we

should be. After years of trying to break through in the UK, we were determined that any new band would not make the same mistakes. Glenn Wheatley had some good contacts with American record companies and we made the American market our number-one priority. I didn't realise it at the time but that meeting offered me probably the last opportunity to grasp the 'brass ring' of success.

I was non-committal at the time but we made an agreement to convene in Melbourne in early 1975 and to give it a try. After years of banging my head against a brick wall in England, I was planning to return to Australia anyway and I thought I might have a future in the business as a manager or agent. The money I had earned with Cliff would pay my fare home (thank you, Sir Cliff!).

I went to Irene and told her what was happening and she gave me her blessing to go. I said she should join me later when she had raised the money. We both had next to no savings; in fact, none. Within a year, I would write her a 'Dear John' letter ending our relationship. I knew I hurt her and I regretted that, but I was in love with someone else.

In September 1974, almost twenty years to the day after I left England with my family for the first time, I boarded an Air India Boeing 707 with a few personal items packed in a trunk. After bidding a tearful goodbye to my girlfriend, and to England in general, the plane took off from Heathrow Airport and into the night.

Recalling that day, I couldn't get Elton John's 'Daniel' out of my head. I felt sad, but secretly relieved, to be finally heading home.

Circa 1974: I was ready to return home to Australia after years of banging my head against a brick wall when Glenn Wheatley and the guys from Mississippi called. (Courtesy Geoff Hales)

CHAPTER 10

It's a (very) Long Way There

W hen I left England, I had bought the cheapest ticket I could afford – first stop Moscow! – and hours later, we landed to refuel. The airport was covered in snow and the plane seemed to be guarded by armed soldiers but we did not get out of the terminal. Another five hours and I was in Bombay, I think, or was it New Delhi? The following day we landed in Sydney, the passengers welcomed by two quarantine officers who sprayed us as we sat in our seats, as was the custom in those days.

I had forgotten how brilliant the light was in Sydney. As the taxi crossed the Harbour Bridge towards Kirribilli, I was plunged into a wonderful September spring morning. I had arranged to stay a short while with Sue Holland, a friend of Irene's and mine, who had hosted many a smoky soirée back in her flat on the Fulham Road. One of the first things I did was to go to the milk bar across the busy road and order a pie and a lime milkshake whisked in the traditional aluminium beakers. I knew then I was back where I belonged.

After a week in Sydney sleeping off the jet lag, I completed my homecoming journey to Adelaide and was reunited with my family in the hairdryer heat of Elizabeth. For a short time, we were a family again. My first Christmas back in Australia

Roger McLachlan and yours truly in the newly convened Little River Band, 1975. Chick magnets? You don't see many neckerchiefs any more.

coincided with the destruction of Cyclone Tracy, which flattened Darwin on Christmas Eve and led to the greatest loss of life on Australian soil since World War II. Adelaide actually took in many of the refugees.

Graeham Goble was back with his family in the Adelaide suburb of Fullarton South and I would go over there and work on some songs together. I had demos of 'Help Is On Its Way', 'Emma', 'Statue Of Liberty' and 'Seine City' which ended up on our first album, so I was fairly well prepared if we did become a band.

I also caught up with old friends and colleagues, sitting in with the Mount Lofty Rangers, a band that was known as Fraternity before I left for England, with Bon Scott as their lead singer. Bon's close friend Vince Lovegrove (ex-Valentines) was managing a club called Countdown, of all things, at the Mediterranean Hotel in the city and I did a Sunday afternoon 'welcome home' gig there with a make-up band whose drummer was John Swan, the older brother of Jimmy Barnes.

I was pleased Adelaide had not forgotten me and Vince gave me a lot of encouragement in the articles he wrote for *Juke* magazine, but Melbourne was where I had to be. Glenn Wheatley arrived back in Australia and he and his wife Alison were staying with Jim Keays, the lead singer of the Masters Apprentices, in suburban Carlton. Glenn arranged for me to lodge at the home of one of Jim's neighbour, a naturopath to the rock 'n' roll crowd. So, I said goodbye again to ever-loving Adelaide, my musical hometown and headed off to Melbourne.

Jim Keays was trying to reinvent himself in a Bowie style alter ego in the guise of 'The Boy from the Stars', complete with a winged mercury helmet. He was to launch the new concept in the prestigious Dallas Brooks Hall in East Melbourne, lowered onto the stage, in full alien style, in a Perspex capsule. Jim asked me and Marcia Hines to sing backup for him at the gig. The venue did not have theatre staging or wing facilities so there was nowhere to lower the 'Boy from the Stars' from. Brave Jim was undeterred; the promoters flooded the stage with smoke and, in the dark, roadies would carry the capsule on and Jim would creep unseen into it shrouded in the smoke.

Unfortunately, the smoke machine malfunctioned thereby the whole process was displayed without any effect whatsoever. Jim crept across the stage in full view (albeit in the gloom) and entered the space ship, the lights came up and he walked out as if he had just arrived on earth! It was a classic *Spinal Tap* moment, if ever I saw one. Marcia and I almost wet our pants (drummer Geoff Cox lost it and dropped his sticks). To Jim's credit, he took it all in his stride. He was the eternal optimist which served him well in later years battling multiple myeloma, which he finally succumbed to in 2014. Vale Jim Keays!

As one of the three singers in the new band, I began working in an acoustic fashion with Gracham and Beeb. Working on Graeham's 'It's A Long Way There' helped develop our signature sound. We also auditioned bass players and lead guitarists while Glenn Wheatley met with record companies.

Our band was taking shape in crude rehearsal surroundings in a disused bakery in North Melbourne. Dave Orams was our original bass player, but we settled on New Zealander Roger McLachlan, who had played in the touring band for the musical *Godspell*. Roger was a tall, good-looking guy who played great bass. He was an affable guy who I got on well with so we decided to move in together and share the rent.

Lead guitarist Graham Davidge was from Adelaide but after moving to Melbourne to work with us he didn't dig Graeham's meticulous approach to the music and left after a couple of rehearsal sessions. We settled on Italian-born Canadian Rick Formosa, which meant Graeham was the only Australian-born member of the band (Beeb being Dutch, real name Gerard Bertlekamp, and Derek Pellicci and me being ten-pound Poms). Shades of Esperanto!

I was eager to get a repertoire together so we could perform live and start earning some money. Graeham, Beeb and Derek, however, wanted to refine every nuance of our music and rush into the recording studio which caused me, as the lead singer, no end of frustration. They made it clear, however, that if we were to continue together as a group then, this was how we would do it ... we'd cross the t's and dot the i's and sing the thing eighty-four times!

'If you don't like it,' Graeham said to me at the time, 'you can leave.' Really? He was prepared to play that card so early? I had obviously pressed a button and I got the heads-up very early that it was Graeham's band and Beeb and Derek would fall in behind him. I went along with them even though I felt we should have done a few live gigs to get some songs together and hang out with each other.

This was to be the first inkling of the inner workings of LRB. I bit my tongue and suffered long and hard with the constant tune ups, drum checks and equipment trials which quickly became the norm in the band.

At my suggestion we developed a cover version of the Everly Brothers' 'When Will I Be Loved' and recorded it at Armstrong Studios in Melbourne in February. We did a great job changing the two-part harmonies to three-part and it was going to be our first single. Unfortunately, Linda Ronstadt's version appeared in the charts in March. I remember someone in the band came into the studio and said, 'Have you heard Linda Ronstadt's new song?'

'What? No, shit!'

Our version was quickly shelved (featuring Graham Davidge on guitar, it would not see the light of day until a 1988 rarities album, *Too Late To Load*).

I was also never comfortable with the band being named after an American river. Mississippi? Was that what we wanted to be? As Glenn Wheatley recounts in his memoir:

> It was now time to get out of the rehearsal room and play to a live audience – somewhere without any fanfare, somewhere out of the way. I booked the Golfview Hotel in Geelong for the Saturday night of 1 March 1975. While travelling to the venue down the Geelong Road from Melbourne, we passed the turn-off for Little River. From the back of the truck, Glenn Shorrock shouted, "What about the Little River Band?" And so, that night the Golfview Hotel witnessed the first performance of the Little River Band, albeit advertised on the marquee as Mississippi.'

I had said Little River sounded like a song title and immediately suggested we should be called the Little River Band. It ticked all the boxes – it's an egalitarian, organic name; it's international (there's a Little River everywhere) and gave kudos to the guys from Mississippi while forging a more modest, self-effacing identity.

Little River Band fitted beautifully, although it was a bit of a tongue twister for a lot of DJs and eventually was simplified to LRB. We tried a few other names, which didn't stick, and we kept coming back to the Little River Band. Eventually, we all agreed to it. For years I've told the joke that if we had gone a mile further down the road we could have called ourselves Wrong Way Go Back or even Men At Work!

We made our public debut as Little River Band on a Sunday afternoon, 20 March 1975. The venue was called Martini's and we did a couple of sets of covers, old Mississippi songs, and showcased our new material. It was an encouraging start. Songs like 'It's A Long Way There', 'My Lady And Me' and 'Meanwhile' worked well alongside covers such as 'Ramblin' Man', 'Drift Away' and Little Feat's 'Dixie Chicken'! I seem to remember doing 'Needle In A Haystack' as well and we got a rewarding reception from friends, family members and even some paying customers.

Things began to fall into place fairly quickly. Little River Band quickly gained a reputation as a live act and more and more gigs came our way. We also employed two roadies who owned a Dodge truck, Mick Lillie and Grant Walsh, who became part of our growing concern and worked their bums off up and down the country.

One story comes to mind from the early LRB days and concerns a show we played on the back of a truck on the oval of the Pakenham South Football Club in an area of Victoria known as Gippsland, on the Princess Highway, on the way to the Latrobe Valley. It wasn't the most exotic place to perform, passing hamlets called Koo Wee Rup and Nar Nar Goon, but this particular day cold, windy showers came across from the 'Bight' and the temperature was down to single figures on the Celsius scale.

Sharing the bill with us that night was AC/DC, also in their fledgling period. There was little production by them back then, just a rented PA system and five young blokes on stage with fashionably long hair. I knew their lead singer Bon Scott from his Valentines days and upon arrival I was told by a roadie that he was in the football club change rooms getting dressed for the gig.

I found Bon sitting on a bench with his trousers off, pouring sand into a sock, ostensibly to exaggerate his power 'bulge'.

'What are you doing?' I enquired.

'The chicks fucking love it man,' he replied with a wide-eyed grin, and offered me a hit from his bottle of 'Jack'.

Thanks for the memory, Bon.

The pub scene had taken over in Melbourne in 1975 and we worked far and wide, from Sunshine to Frankston and beyond. One of our favourite gigs was Sunday afternoons at the Station Hotel in Greville Street, Prahran, which always had a friendly vibe with close proximity between audience and band. Roger McLachlan and I exploited that proximity with our female fans; our après-show parties were a great way to wind up a busy week!

All that was to quickly change.

In May 1975, we opened for Leo Sayer at Melbourne's Festival Hall. Unbeknown to me, in the audience that night was my dear friend Gael McKay, back home from the UK and watching the concert with a girlfriend, Jo Swan. The next day we were in Studio 2 at Armstrong's in Banks Street, South Melbourne to start recording our first album. AAV (Armstrong Audio Video) was the cutting-edge recording facility at the time, situated on three floors and catering for audio and video production.

During the day, I was sent a note saying that a friend of Gael's was working upstairs and they had been at the previous night's concert. I went to find out more of Gael's whereabouts and met Jo, a gregarious pretty young woman. I asked about Gael and she told me that she'd left for a photographic assignment. We talked for a short time and we felt a spark.

We were both working in the same building, me in the basement studio and she in video production on the third floor, so we began seeing each other during the day and eventually she gave me a lift home in her VW. We kissed and you probably know the rest. Jo later became my wife and, more than forty years later, she is still by my side.

Back in '75, we went out together a few times but she said she wanted to return to England and travel. I was still technically seeing another woman but I soon realised Jo was the one I had to be with. We both liked to laugh, dance, have sex and drink wine ... sometimes all at once!

Jo was twenty-two when I met her and I was thirty-one. Three years before, she had left Australia with her best friend Peta on their journey of discovery. Sailing to Singapore on the Greek liner *Patris*, they then flew Olympus Airlines to Athens and on to Mykonos where they lived for several months. Jo masqueraded as a Greek dancer for visiting cruise ships and worked in a taverna with Peta, eventually making their way to London.

Her then boyfriend Tony, persuaded her to join him in Thailand so the two then flew to Kathmandu where Jo got ill with dysentery before managing to make her way to India and Pakistan. They then bused across the border through the Khyber Pass into Afghanistan. Tony left for London and Jo flew Aeroflot through Moscow, the cheapest way, back to London, where she got a job with an advertising company in 1971 when video was becoming the new medium.

Jo met up again with her teenage friend, Gael McKay, while they were both working there, which means we were both in London at that same time, with a mutual friend, but never met until we returned to Australia.

******

With our past reputations in Zoot, Mississippi, Twilight and Axiom, Glenn Wheatley had little difficulty in securing LRB a record deal with EMI in Sydney, with a little help from Stephen Shrimpton, Managing Director, who became our willing champion in that crucial beginning of the group.

Our first single, Beeb's 'Curiosity (Killed The Cat)', was released in September 1975. The song was very commercial, with a great bassline and a cool groove, peaking at number fifteen on the Australian charts. Because we had written all the material ourselves, we produced our self-titled debut album rather than bringing in an outside producer. EMI went ballistic when we went over budget by $2000, but once it was released in November, the company more than got their money's worth, with the record eventually going gold.

Four of my songs were included on that first self-titled album: 'Statue Of Liberty', which of course had been recorded by Esperanto, 'Meanwhile ...', 'The Man In Black' and 'Emma', the latter being added to the album at the last moment and was released as our second single that Christmas. The stand-out track on the album was the nine-minute anthem 'It's A Long Way There', with a signature guitar solo from Rick Formosa that was recorded at his first attempt. The following year, an edited version of that song would be our first US release.

The less said about the terrible cover art on the album the better – caricatures of the band with bubble heads driving down a country road. It was bloody awful but at least the Americans had the good sense to replace it with a photo of the band when it was released there later.

The flow of the Little River Band accelerated quickly during that first year. Our main rivals at that time were Sherbet and Skyhooks. Although they had a UK hit with 'Howzat', Sherbet were on the wane from their pop heyday but the 'Hooks were very much on the rise. We shared the bill occasionally that first year and got on really well with them, especially their lead singer Graeme 'Shirley' Strachan. I liked their on-stage theatrical personas (especially Red Symons), as I did the guys in Split Enz, who had crossed the 'dutch' from New Zealand around the same time.

Ian 'Molly' Meldrum's music program *Countdown* premiered that year on the ABC (in colour!) and Australian music received a great boost thanks to the exposure it gave us all on Sunday nights. From his early days as a writer for *Go-Set* magazine Molly was always the greatest supporter for Oz music but *Countdown* took this to a new level.

At the end of 1975, Glenn Wheatley travelled to Los Angeles and touted the group to various record companies. He faced resistance from some labels (one record executive reportedly described our sound as 'fingernails running down the blackboard'!)

Overleaf: Little River Band on stage in an early TV performance in 1976. David Briggs (far left) and George McArdle (next to him) have joined the band, completing the line-up that achieved our greatest success. Derek often liked to drum shirtless. (Courtesy Bob King)

Graeham and me on
the phone to Florida
DJ Bill Bartlett in 1976
as Glenn Wheatley
looks on. Bill was one
of the first people in
the US to champion our
music on radio.

but then not everyone hated of our high-pitched vocals. Capitol Records' Rupert Perry liked what we were doing and signed us to a three-year deal on Christmas Eve 1975. EMI Australia released us from our contract with their good wishes, largely because of the intervention of Stephen Shrimpton, who was destined for his own international success as head of Paul McCartney's group of companies and then CEO of Warner Music International.

I had a hit record, I was in love and there was some money in my pocket at last! What could go wrong? I seem to have heard that before. Already the wind of change was blowing through LRB.

CHAPTER 11

LRB in the USA

L ife was changing rapidly.

In 1976, Little River Band recorded our second album, *After Hours*, which was released in May and remains my favourite of all the LRB albums. The band really found its sound on that album. It has an eclectic mix of songs with an organic thread running through it. On the back of a hell of a lot of local touring, the album peaked at number five on the Australian charts and produced a top-thirty single, Beeb's 'Everyday Of My Life'.

Unfortunately, it wasn't an altogether happy experience making the album, with tensions in the studio between the three main songwriters coming to a head. With everyone in the band needing to agree that a song was album worthy, there was a lot of politicking going on within the band. Only two of my songs made the cut, the aforementioned 'Seine City' and 'Sweet Old Fashioned Man', and I started to think twice about putting my songs forward to Beeb and Graeham, who were pushing hard for their songs to be included.

Rick Formosa then decided to leave during the recording of this album. He had studied music in the Milan and wanted to pursue more serious musical endeavours rather than touring and playing live with a 'pop band'. He left us with some fine guitar performances and a great song, 'Bourbon Street', on this album (he also co-wrote the song 'Another Runway' with Beeb). He also contributed some great arrangements (and would continue to do

LRB in London in 1976 before we headed off to the US on our first tour. We supported the Hollies on their European tour before going to London and playing some gigs there ... eighteen months earlier the four key members of the band were living there, pretty much penniless.

so for LRB) but for me, his legacy was turning me on to the American band Little Feat, but more about that later.

For some reason, Graeham and Derek took Ric's decision to leave as a cue to get rid of Roger McLachlan as our bass player. Unknown to Rog and me, while we were in Sydney doing promotional work for the band, the other members of the band had already found his replacement. Graeham, Derek and Beeb had been recommended David Briggs as a possible guitarist, and went to the Pink Pussycat club in Melbourne to check him out playing in a funk band called the Ram Band. Bassist George McArdle was playing in the same band.

Graeham and Derek then decided to replace Roger with George McArdle, who they thought was a better player. To make matters worse, Jo and I had just moved into a house with Roger in Windsor with two of Jo's girlfriends. I was completely taken by surprise when Roger was told by Glenn Wheatley – over the phone, what's more – that his services would no longer be required.

I voiced my opinion but I got little support from the other members of the band. 'What do you mean Roger's out,' I protested. 'He's our bass player, and he's a great team player too.' We were having success with Roger so I didn't see the need for change; never mind the loyalty aspect, which has always been important to me. I was to learn otherwise about these issues.

The 'revolving door' policy in the band would become a real problem for me as far as band unity was concerned. I thought that changing the bass player was more a sign that the others felt insecure with themselves but, once again, I had to compromise. The message was clear: 'If you don't like it, leave.'

George McArdle and David Briggs had two weeks to learn two albums' worth of songs before we left for our first overseas tour. George is a lovely guy, and he was a great player too, possessing a great 'thumb slap' technique popular with American jazz players. Roger later joined country-rock pioneers Stars and became a

Winter in America (thank you Doug Ashdown) … we're cold but we're smiling; the novelty yet to wear off.

much-sought-after session player. Although George changed the dynamic of our rhythm section for the better, the great irony is, he would ultimately leave the band of his own accord.

On the upside, things were moving quickly for us. *After Hours* was doing well at home and we embarked on a tour up the east coast to Cairns. Glenn Wheatley was setting up offices in South Melbourne and one in Marina del Rey in LA, incorporating Tumbleweed Music, OZ Records and Wheatley Brothers Entertainment. We were now incorporated! The American market became a priority and all strategies were aimed there.

EMI England, being label 'cousins' of Capital, wanted to get us over for a promotional tour to open for the Hollies. Our tour in Europe was great and we got on well with the Hollies; after all,

they had been an influence on us and our shows were dripping with similar harmonies. Graeham and Beeb were huge fans of the band and I hit it off immediately with my lead singer counterpart Allan Clarke, who years earlier had taken notice of the Twilights' version of his song 'What's Wrong With The Way I Live'.

Days later, we found ourselves back in London but holding a better hand of cards than during our previous time there. We played the Marquee Club in London again before travelling to the Chapman Theatre at Salford University, Manchester the following night. We then left for the USA.

A young LA booking agent named John Marx had fallen in love with our record and hounded Glenn to represent us. His brother Chuck had a small company called Headquarters and we chose them over the big companies because of their enthusiasm for the band. I didn't know it at the time but we had only three shows booked ahead of us when we arrived in the US. John and Glenn Wheatley were still working on our itinerary but they did a great job securing gigs for us in various colleges, clubs and yes, stadiums.

In October 1976, I finally landed in the country whose music and culture has influenced me since I was a twelve-year-old. We flew into Dulles Airport in Washington DC, including our road crew of one, manager Glenn Wheatley. Two American roadies met us there with two rented station wagons and we drove into Virginia to play our first gig at Madison College in Harrisburg, supporting the Average White Band.

Within half an hour of leaving the airport we were pulled over by a motorcycle cop who seemed interested in our cars loaded with a bunch of hairy guys and so much luggage. It was as if I was in a scene from a road movie; the cop came complete with reflective Ray Ban sunglasses and laden with various weapons and radio paraphernalia. We tried to explain ourselves in our thick Australian accents, which confused the cop so much he waved us away and wished us luck as we continued on our merry way. Welcome to America!

That first night, we were halfway through our set in the college gym when the power failed and Derek played a solo for what seemed like an eternity until the power came back on and we could continue. When we finished, the crowd gave us a standing ovation and we looked at each other, as if to say, 'This won't be so difficult after all.'

The Average White Band were great to work with and also very complimentary to us. They were from England and new kids on the block too, and formed an affinity with us from the start.

LRB in front of No.10 Downing Street, the British Prime Minister's residence. Harold Wilson was the Prime Minister at the time but if he was home that day he was not taking visitors … not from an Australian rock 'n' roll band anyway.

From there, it was all a bit of a blur ... highways, motels, radio interviews, colleges, small clubs and more highways. We played almost fifty dates in the US over the next three months before returning home just before Christmas. The band were kept buoyant by the sound of 'It's A Long Way There' playing on the radio as we crisscrossed the country. The song eventually reached number twenty-eight and we were on our way.

The 'fire' under LRB was lit by a Florida FM radio station in Jacksonville, Florida; specifically, programming manager Bill Bartlett who loved this new 'Aussie' music, especially LRB and AC/DC. We were treated like real rock stars when we arrived at Jacksonville for two nights in the middle of November and played

Recording *Diamantina
Cocktail* with producer
John Boylan and
engineer Ross Cockle
(both on right) in
1977. The album,
the first with John,
was recorded at AAV
Studios in South
Melbourne and went
on to become the
highest grossing album
in Australia that year.

to 2000 fans. I was finally achieving something I'd thought about for years. Success in America.

We got to LA and did the necessary pressing of the flesh with the guys at Capitol and numerous interviews, and there seemed to be a genuine buzz about the band. We stayed at the Sunset Marquis, just off Sunset Boulevard, which was to become our go-to destination in the coming years.

I shared a room with David Briggs, the other smoker in the band, who was even more excited than me about soaking up the Southern Californian culture. The Sunset was an apartment hotel built around a swimming pool and was used by other ambitious ladder climbers like us. I loved staying there. The next rung up as far as accommodation went was the Hyatt Hotel or 'Riot House' as it was known, around the corner.

The reality of working in the US lived up to all my expectations. I wish I could say it was a hard slog with many setbacks but our entry into the music scene in America was really quite smooth. Our radio-friendly sound was perfect for the times and we consistently backed it up with our live performances. Someone on tour once asked me, 'How come you sound so much like your records?' To which I replied. 'Whose records do you want us to sound like?'

Being an Australian band was a good point of difference for us when talking to the media but we never courted publicity. We let our music do the talking. LRB was sometimes tagged as a British band by the American press as our sound was an international one. 'How come you guys speak such good English?' some reporters asked us, thinking we were Austrian instead of Australian! We had fun taking the micky out of some unenlightened interviewers on that tour.

I was always conscious of the fact that we were working in the country that invented pop culture. Pop music is one of the most popular of the arts but the least revered but we cherished being part of that heritage. Some nitpickers asked why we sang in an

American accent. The answer was because that's how we heard
it. If rock 'n' roll had been a Polish phenomenon we would have
been singing in Polish accents!

LRB didn't really comply with the public perception of life
on the road as being filled with wild goings on but we did have
our moments, usually instigated by the crew, although certain
members of the band would join in the shenanigans. In the early
hours of one cold, clear morning, plastic rubbish bins were seen
arching through the night sky, propelled by pyrotechnics. Alcohol
was the predominant relaxant but soft recreational drugs were
used throughout those days by different members of the touring
party. I of course monitored their use!

One reviewer in Spokane, Washington described me as the 'irrepressible Troy Donahue lookalike George Shark!' From that day on I've been known as 'Sharky' by my intimates. The rest of the review was littered with mistakes too, so maybe the guy hadn't even been at the concert at all.

Our return to Melbourne just before Christmas 1976 was an orchestrated publicity event complete with our first press conference. We basked in our new notoriety but then Jo and I drove off in our old VW, which came to a halt halfway down the road home, while the press sped by. There's no business like ...

Capitol felt we should have a producer work with us on our next record and John Boylan came down to Melbourne to meet with the band. Straight away we hit it off with John, an erudite New England college guy just a little older than me with a good pedigree in the music business. When we learnt he had been influential in the early careers of the Eagles and Linda Ronstadt, and he had just had a huge hit as the producer of Boston's 'More Than A Feeling,' we knew we couldn't have had a better guy to guide us into the US recording industry. Plus, he thought our songs were 'killer'!

As well as being a fine producer, John Boylan became another huge influence in my life and we became great friends. I was his 'little buddy' and he was a conduit to my understanding of the academic side of life the US. When Jo and I married in 1980, I chose John as my best man and his home in Nichols Canyon in LA became the place for us to visit for years to come. We enjoyed his bon vivant company throughout my days on the road. Châteauneuf-du-Pape was his favourite red and we enjoyed many a bottle together over the years.

We recorded our third album *Diamantina Cocktail* in February 1977. I think Derek Pellicci came up with the name – he tended to name all the early albums – and he found out about this bush drink from the Diamantina River in Queensland consisting of Bundaberg Rum, condensed milk and an emu egg! The album

LRB in front of our tour bus on the 1978–79 northern winter tour of the USA. This is one of my favourite pictures of the band, perhaps best reflecting the fellowship of touring for weeks on end, but that winter probably broke George McArdle. He left LRB at the end of the tour.

cover featured the band in colonial dress, complete with band mascot Skittles the bulldog, which evoked the colonial era.

Released in April, the album sold 100,000 copies at home, reaching number two on the national charts, but it was the highest selling album of 1977. The $150,000 Capitol spent on it was easily recouped.

The first single from the album was 'Help Is On Its Way', which became our first number-one hit in Australia, was also named Australian Record of the Year for 1977 and earned me Best Australian Songwriter award. 'Help Is On Its Way' features a great opening bass line from George McArdle, who instinctively joined in when I was playing an early version of the song on the studio piano. The song was also the first of ten top-twenty hits for us in the US.

'Witchery', written by Graeham and Beeb, and which started life as a jingle for the retail clothing chain some years before, was released as the follow up to 'Help Is On Its Way' in Australia but was not a huge success. Conversely, 'Happy Anniversary Baby', written by Beeb and David Briggs, was the second single released off the album in the US and became another top-twenty hit.

We commenced our second tour of the US in May 1977 in support of our album release the following month. Capitol hadn't thought *After Hours* strong enough to release in the crowded US market so they made the decision to combine some of the stronger songs from that record with *Diamantina Cocktail*, which made the new album an even better product. It became our breakthrough album on AM radio right across the United States. *Diamantina Cocktail* was the first Australian album to sell half a million copies in the US.

Canada, Japan, Holland and Germany began to bubble along too, though not so much England, but the next two years were life changing for me. In August 1977 we flew to England and supported Aerosmith and the Doobie Brothers at the Reading Rock Festival, in what could only be described as a sea of mud. On

A publicity shot featuring the front cover of our breakthrough album *Diamantina Cocktail* in 1977. Graphic artists Jo Ford and Ray Wilkinson did the iconic design and art direction, even finding a place for Skittles, their canine mascot.

LITTLE RIVER BAND

MANAGEMENT GLENN WHEATLEY
325 MORAY STREET
SOUTH MELBOURNE 3205
699 5366

11 November 1977, we supported Fleetwood Mac and Santana at the Rockarena concert at Sydney Showground, drawing a crowd in excess of 40,000 people. Two days later, 70,000 fans turned out at Melbourne's Calder Raceway. We had left Australia as a club act and returned at the end of 1977 as stadium headliners.

For the first time, I was earning decent money too. So much so, that the band's accountant advised us all to go out and 'buy a house, a car and a boat!' Jo and I gladly obeyed. We found an Edwardian house in Albert Park, Melbourne, bought an Alfa Romeo GTV and a Bertram 28-foot cruiser, housed at St Kilda Marina, all in that same year. I liked money but had little interest or experience in earning or handling it. Luckily, I come from a reasonably normal background where wealth played second fiddle to happiness and pleasure.

Jo was working at the Campaign Palace advertising agency as a producer and the creative team at 'the Palace' were used to long lunches in the burgeoning bistros of the area. I became a willing participant when I wasn't touring. Strong friendships were forged at the time that continue to this day.

Sitting with Jo at LAX international airport and reading news of the death of Elvis in August 1977. The look on my face says it all. (Courtesy Beeb Birtles)

******

In December 1976, LRB stayed at the Las Vegas Hilton when we played the Convention Centre there. We just missed Elvis, who had recently ended his Las Vegas run. I was missing Jo and doodling on some Hilton stationery, and came up with the lines:

I'll be home on a Monday,
somewhere around noon,
please don't be angry,
I'll be back with you real soon.

Beeb contributed the middle eight, 'You looked so lovely when I left I nearly didn't go, twelve thousand miles …' and the resulting song, 'Home On A Monday' would take on a new poignancy the following year.

Fast-forward to 16 August, 1977, and news that Elvis Presley is dead, at the age of forty-two, stuns the world. The next day, LRB played the Aladdin Theatre in Las Vegas.

Overleaf: Playing to a packed Opera House in February 1978 … our own crowded House!

Elvis' death in 1977 brought a new meaning to the lines from 'Home On A Monday':

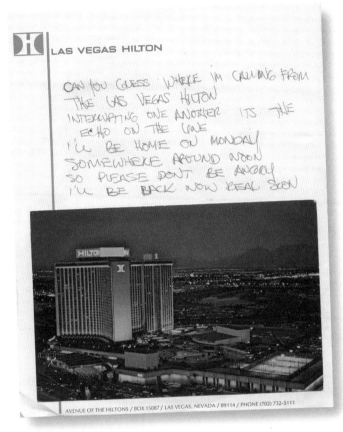

LAS VEGAS HILTON

CAN YOU GUESS WHERE I'M CALLING FROM
THE LAS VEGAS HILTON
INTERRUPTING ONE ANOTHER ITS THE
ECHO ON THE LINE
I'LL BE HOME ON MONDAY
SOMEWHERE AROUND NOON
SO PLEASE DON'T BE ANGRY
I'LL BE BACK NOW REAL SOON

AVENUE OF THE HILTONS / BOX 15087 / LAS VEGAS, NEVADA / 89114 / PHONE (702) 732-5111

My handwritten lyrics for 'Home On A Monday', scribbled on Las Vegas Hilton stationery while I talked to Jo on the phone.

I was hoping to catch a glimpse,
of the man from Memphis,
they told me that he had gone,
never leaving a trace.

It was a pivotal event in all our lives ... what a shock, what a waste!

Like so many others, I had watched Elvis' slow decline into the caricature that often represents him to this day, but when he died I immediately thought about his effect on me back in 1956: hearing 'Heartbreak Hotel'; the dark brooding roles in films *Jailhouse Rock* and *King Creole*, and that wonderful image of him in *Loving You* singing 'Teddy Bear' in that fabulous red and white, Roy Rogers-style satin shirt. Unfortunately, Elvis let his manager Colonel Tom Parker have his way and he settled for being a cheesy matinée idol. But for a long while, he was the rock god the rest of us wanted to emulate.

I agree with John Lennon when he said that 'Without Elvis there would never have been the Beatles'. Damn right! Elvis had it all.

And for a time in my teenage years, I loved him.

CHAPTER 12

Reminiscing

In the late seventies everything seemed to grow exponentially for LRB. And so began our routine of album, tour, tour, album, tour, tour. We travelled more, played more venues and reached more people with our music than any other Australian band. As a result, our record sales increased and financially we were all thrust into uncharted territory.

To have success, and then get paid so well for it, was not taken lightly be me. Throughout my life, I have acknowledged that I've been very fortunate with my lot and I was eager to enjoy my luck.

In May 1978, just weeks before we headed off to the US to promote our new album *Sleeper Catcher,* Derek Pellicci was badly burned in an accident at a barbeque. I wasn't there that day but we were told that Derek had ducked away to visit his father in hospital and when he returned they tried to restart the fire and he was badly burned by a bottle of methylated spirits. He suffered third-degree burns on his face, neck and chest and ended up in the same hospital as his dad. There were real concerns that he wouldn't recover, let alone play the drums again.

The great irony is, Derek was the hypochondriac in the band to the point where you never asked him how he was feeling on tour. When we visited Derek in hospital he was in a bad way, with his face badly bloated, and he spent the next few months in hospital. Rather than cancelling shows for the US tour,

In a pool, stateside in Dallas, wearing a 'Super Test' bucket hat (on me bucket head!) which was given to me by Dennis Lillee in the late 1970s.

147

Geoff Cox, a former drummer with Brian Cadd, substituted on drums. The show must go on.

I enjoyed Geoff's company on the road but months later, we were overjoyed to see Derek standing in the wings at our gig in Toronto, Canada, surprising us all with his early return from hospital. Geoff Cox played alongside Derek for a few gigs, doubling on drums, until Derek was strong enough to continue on his own.

Like *Diamantina Cocktail, Sleeper Catcher* was another Australia-themed title, being named after the person who holds and collects the money during the gambling game two-up. The album sold 100,000 copies at home, peaking at number three, but went on to become the first Australian album to sell a million copies in the US.

My song, 'Shut Down Turn Off' was the highest charting of the four singles off the album in Australia and is typical of the musical era, with a distinctive synth-drum beat. In the US, however, the big hit was Graeham Goble's 'Reminiscing', which peaked at number on the Billboard charts in June 1978. 'Reminiscing' also has reached five million airplays on American radio, which is a record for an Aussie song.

No-one in the band thought it was a potential single, the American record company picked it out. '"Reminiscing"? Really?' Graeham recalls that he had resistance from the band about recording the song from the start but I don't remember that. I loved the song from the outset and I thought we did a great job on the complicated, five-part harmonies. It's a clever melody with some sophisticated guitar chords, although I didn't think it was too relevant at the time, given what was happening what with disco and punk battling it out at the time, but there you go.

Graeham loved the music of the Glenn Miller Band and the rest of that era, as did I. 'Walking in the park, dancing in the dark ...' it's just a lovely, nostalgic song. The promotional

LRB in 1978. Derek wasn't an AFL fan per se but he liked to wear sleeveless Aussie Rules jerseys on stage because it provided him with the freedom to drum. This jersey is of the old South Melbourne club, which later became the Sydney Swans in the early 1980s, and the club got in touch with Glenn Wheatley to thank us for our support (they used to play 'Help Is On Its Way' whenever the team kicked a goal!). They've been my favourite team ever since.

Overleaf: On stage at the Sydney Opera House in 1978. A triumphant return from the US for the band.

film clip we made for 'Reminiscing' was similarly atmospheric and nostalgic. Melbourne socialite and racing enthusiastic Peter Janson had an apartment on the top floor at the Hotel Windsor. We moved in for a couple of days and had some fun filming the clip surrounded by his various toys – knights in shining armour, stuffed polar bears and an antique poor table.

In June 1978 we left for America on another national tour but this time we would also be headliners. Now, when we travelled internationally by plane we turned left when we boarded, towards the front of the plane. We travelled mostly by plane on those early tours but we soon found that buses were much better. The 'stage coaches' had been popular with country artists for years as their homes away from home and now the rock 'n' roll people had started using them too. At one period we were using three buses in total, each accommodating up to a dozen people.

The buses could sleep twelve people along the centre, bookended between two lounges, one up front with kitchenette and loo, and a rear one for hanging out watching TV and movies. One bus was the designated party bus so I was on that one of course. The families filled one bus; the bus I travelled on had a strong fragrance around it but the crew's bus could be smelt from some distance away. I had some great times on the road with the band and more so with the crew, who were a large part of our success.

Our touring party grew to about thirty people over the years and included my 'road buddy', Peter Rooney, our lighting director (later relieved by Chris Newman) and my 'minder'. Our front of house sound engineer was Grant Walsh (also my original minder) to begin with and then Ernie Rose took over for the band's halcyon days, so our sound was never compromised and gained us respect from our peers. Guys like John Money, Michael Wickow and John Bishop also deserve a lot of credit, as do so many others who have shared the road with me.

Thank you, boys! And thank you too to the guy that guided

me to my room while carrying a small palm I'd ripped out of its pot in the lobby of the Grand Hotel in Kansas City and putting us both to bed!

I enjoyed sleeping on my bunk with the curtain closed for privacy with a good road book (Stephen King was a favourite author back then). I liked the feeling of lying on my back, feet first and a metre and a half off the ground, travelling at 100 kilometres an hour (and with an illegal smile on my face!). One of our favourite things to do was to check out all the numerous amusement parks dotted all over the States (on hot summer days, Wet and Wild was the go!).

A typical day on the road usually began waking up as the bus pulled into a motel somewhere in Bum-fuck Idaho or such. I would fall out of my bunk, was handed my room key by the tour manager and, depending on the time of day, I would look for food and then retire to my room, sleep some more and wake around 5 pm ready to be bussed to the sound check. The caterer

Fooling around on the drums during a sound check.

would serve the evening meal most of the time; if not we would be back to the hotel for a shower and a snack.

The show of course came next; a ninety minute to two-hour set followed by a 'meet and greet' with the record people, radio and media. We'd drink the 'rider' (mostly alcohol), leaving some for the crew, and then load the rest onto the bus and head off into the night and on to the next town, which was sometimes 300 miles away. We'd arrive at the next hotel around mid-morning, ready for another typical American breakfast of eggs and corned beef hash, sprinkled with Tabasco sauce, and with a helping of beans; the missing ingredient being decent coffee, the 'coffee culture' yet to reach the US.

This routine sometimes could go on for a week to ten days before we were granted a day or two off to rest up and get laundry done. Graeham, on one tour, decided to take an extra bag with him to store his dirties in and returned with them at the end of the tour for his wife to wash at home!

Different techniques were employed by individuals to ease the dynamics of life on the road. Derek would practise packing with a template in his case, marked with designated areas for each type of clothing etc. Upon arrival in a new room, he would throw all the loose hotel paraphernalia into one drawer leaving all surfaces vacant for his stuff in order to affect an easy exit, not leaving anything behind. Clever and effective, but a little too OCD.

Fellowship is a word I've used a lot to describe my attitude to my work. The fellowship I've experienced during my music career is an important part of my journey so far. LRB worked alongside some great artists during our tours of the US and between 1975 and 1982 we shared the stage with some greats of that period such as the Eagles, the Doobie Brothers, Fleetwood Mac, the Beach Boys, Steve Miller Band, Boz Scaggs, Little Feat, Heart, Supertramp, Poco, Dave Mason Band, Jimmy Buffett, Foreigner, America, Bob Seeger, Player, Ambrosia, REO Speedwagon and Edgar Winter.

Pressing the flesh with Capitol executives who came out to present us with gold records for our Australian 'greatest hits' compilation *It's A Long Way There* in 1978. (From left) Don Zimmerman (Capitol), Graeham, George, Derek, SA Premier Don Dunstan, Glenn Wheatley, Steve Shrimpton (EMI), Rupert Perry (Capitol) with Beeb, me and David at the back.

The Doobie Brothers were a particular favourite of ours. We arrived to open for them at a state fair on our first tour without too much equipment with us and they just said to use their gear. Coming from such an accomplished band as them, it was an act of generosity I've never forgotten. But such was the attitude of many American acts of that era, as opposed to the fierce rivalry and home-grown pettiness that we had gotten used to.

LRB opened the door to the US and other Aussie acts came through and made waves on the Californian coastline. In September 1977, we played an uproarious, all-Australian gig in Cleveland with the Dingoes and it was great to catch up with Chris Stockley and the boys. The Dingoes were a band I really admired but they never enjoyed widespread success. We all got drunk together, which made us even more homesick, rather than just sick.

Other colleagues from down under knocking on America's

door had set up base camps in LA – Billy Thorpe, Max Merritt, Russell Morris and, of course, Brian Cadd. Brian was recording for Capitol and was then married to Linda, a vice president of Casablanca Records, so we always met on our stays in LA and continued our friendship.

Billy Thorpe was an intensely powerful performer both on and off stage. We later became much closer when we worked together on his production of *Long Way To The Top* in the new millennium and we were also inducted into the ARIA Hall of Fame in the same year, 1991. We made each other laugh and came to understand each other well.

We were always wary of each other's standing in the music hierarchy, his intensity contrasting starkly with my laissez faire attitude. I got under his skin a little when he and his wife hosted a party in the Hollywood Hills for ex-pat Aussies when LRB was in town in the late 1970s. They were renting a wonderful old 'movie star' home with a swimming pool and I remarked, somewhat disingenuously, 'How can you afford to live like that when you haven't even "made it" yet?' Ouch!

Billy had recorded a space age, psychedelic concept album called *Children Of The Sun* and the title track had taken off in one US state only, Texas. Anyone who had met Thorpie knew that he didn't take a back seat to anyone and we found ourselves on the same bill at a huge concert in the Dallas Cotton Bowl. *Children Of The Sun* had enjoyed airplay in the local area but his billing was behind Fleetwood Mac, REO Speedwagon and LRB, in that order. Billy flat out refused to go on before LRB and made the situation known in his usual subtle way. At this juncture, Glenn Wheatley pointed out that our song 'Reminiscing' was number three nationally on the Billboard charts, which ended the argument then and there. The Dallas gig was most enjoyable due to the fact that it was our biggest ever audience, a mere 86,000 people.

Fleetwood Mac were top dogs at this time, with their 1977

album *Rumours* still selling bucketloads eighteen months later, so their perception of themselves was somewhat 'elevated' shall we say. The message backstage had gone out to the supporting acts to clear the path for the band as each of the five members made their way to the stage in a golf buggy. I can't stand such pretentiousness at the best of times so, fuelled by after-show 'goodies' on offer, I managed to break free of my confinement in our dressing room and, putting on my best Quasimodo impression, I shuffled along beside Ms Nicks' cart entreating her to 'heal me Stevie, heal me.' Needless to say, I was quietly manhandled back inside by security! I did notice, however, that it amused Mick Fleetwood and John McVie, the two hardnosed Englishmen in the band.

Life on the road in America suited me and our success felt very satisfying but it never went to my head. I never thought of LRB as being in the 'A' league but we certainly came close. I suppose what was happening to me was changing me somewhat and maybe I was crossing the line more often. I would say 'I will' rather than 'No, I won't' thereby making a mockery of the term 'willpower'. It must be said, however, that my philosophical leanings now took second place to my desires … and believe me, all my desires were being met.

One of LRB's strong areas was the north-west of the US. Two local bands were Heart and the Steve Miller Band, both of which we hooked up with over the coming years with great results. Steve's band and LRB on the same bill was a very strong show and Nancy and Ann Wilson, the two sisters fronting Heart, were great performers. I think Glenn Wheatley, then happily single, found that out for himself one night in Oregon, although I can't remember with which sister!

Steve Miller was married to an Australian girl at the time (he has been married four times) so he had a real affinity with us. Jo and I spent a lovely day with the Millers on their cruiser on the Seattle Sounds, near his hometown. That part of the States is particularly lovely and the water-loving lifestyle stretches over the

Overleaf: At the Dallas Cotton Bowl before 70,000 fans. It was the biggest stadium we ever played.

border into Canada, especially Vancouver, which became another strong market for LRB. In 1977, we played to over 40,000 people there at Queen Elizabeth Stadium.

Our agent John Marx managed to hook us up with the band Little Feat for a twelve-show run up the west coast. We all loved 'the Feat' and couldn't wait to be on the road with them. I thought we were going to another league when we opened for them ... they were so good you wouldn't want to follow them on a bill. We also thought we could learn a lot from them so, for a dozen or so shows, LRB would open the show and then sit back and wallow in their expertise.

Little Feat, when Lowell George and Bill Payne were fronting them, were the best band I've come across in all my years of being on the road. They were unsung heroes of the American touring scene, and unless you saw them live or played with them – and

Locker room talk before a gig. I can tell his was just after Derek re-joined us in 1978 following his recovery from his accident because he'd grown a beard.

I had the great fortune to do both – it's hard to appreciate just how good they were. They were the real deal, very relaxed on stage and consummate musicians. One night in a sexy deco theatre in Santa Barbara, I found myself watching from the wings, alongside Bonnie Raitt, as the band encored with 'Feats Don't Fail Me Now'. Lowell George (sadly to die, far too young, in 1979) beckoned us both to come on stage to join him around the microphone. I tried my best to keep up and it was vocal heaven for me.

The Band were like that on stage too, just a little looser. I will never forget one magical Sunday afternoon in 1971 at London's Royal Albert Hall when Terry Britten and I were treated to a three-hour, tour de force performance by the Band, who spoke not a word to the audience until the final encore when guitarist Robbie Robertson casually walked up to the microphone and said, 'Good evening.' That was cool.

LRB were confident in our place in the scheme of things. I was constantly blown away by the American bands who were still streets ahead of everyone else but our reputation strengthened among both our fans, and more importantly for me, our peers. We were on a high and playing well; we thought we were a force to be reckoned with having established our credibility with the many bands we were playing alongside. Our gigs were great and we were delivering for our audience.

I had the opportunity to travel over more of the US than most Americans and those years of touring afforded me a 'bus window' view of many of the vistas I'd seen in books as a boy – the bright lights of Vegas, passing herds of bison returning to the prairies of Wyoming, through the St Louis Arch and the Lincoln Tunnel in Manhattan and down to the Louisiana bayous and all the parts in between. It's an amazing nation, the best and the worst of everything.

The rest of the world is good too but 'I still call ...' Well, you know the rest.

CHAPTER 13

The Cracks Begin to Show

On 29 January 1979, LRB played the final concert of our short tour over Christmas and new year headlining the Nambassa Festival in Waihi, New Zealand. Doobie Brother John Hartman doubled on drums with Derek at that gig. The festival drew a crowd of 60,000 people and I remarked at the time that it was the 'last of the Woodstocks' because rock festivals were dead everywhere else.

Rock and roll had grown up since the days of Woodstock and Sunbury and production values for stadium rock in the late 1970s had improved greatly. Not that playing in front of tens of thousands of people fazed me that much. Before a big gig, I'd often be asleep backstage and someone would have to wake me: 'You're on in ten minutes!'

In between songs I would be thinking, 'I've really got to do my laundry tonight!'

That new year tour, however, was the straw that broke the back as far as George McArdle was concerned. Life on the road had not agreed with him and we had just completed a tour in the worst possible conditions – sub-zero temperatures and feet-deep snow wherever we went – in the harsh, Northern Hemisphere winter. While on tour in the US the previous November, Graeham and Beeb had bought him a *Living Bible* for his twenty-fourth birthday. This had a huge impact on George. When Capitol pressed us to sign a new, three-year contract George declined, to our utter

The title of this chapter says it all. I tried to remain my cheery self (ha!) but the cracks were beginning to show.

Produced by John Boylan and Little River Band.
Management: Glenn Wheatley for Wheatley Bros. Entertainment

amazement. He had found God and had decided to leave the band to enrol in a Bible college, with a view to becoming an ecclesiastical pastor. He gave away the rock 'n' roll lifestyle – the fame, the money and the music – to follow God.

We used Clive Harrison in the studio for our next album but Barry Sullivan (ex-Chain and Renée Geyer Band) took over on bass when we again headed off on tour. We also took Renée's keyboard player, former Dingo, Mal Logan, after LRB had toured Australia with Ian Mason the previous year. We struggled for bass players for a while but then we met Wayne Nelson on tour in America and he impressed all of us.

Barry made it clear he didn't want to tour for too long and Wayne joined the band in April 1980. Wayne was from Chicago and was a fine singer and bass player, having played in Jim

This was the billboard of our new album that greeted us on Sunset Boulevard in LA, 1979. A just reward for our success from the people at Capitol and very proud moment for the band. We had well and truly made it in the US, the biggest stage in the world.

FIRST _____ THE WIRE
UNDER

Messina's band. We hit it off immediately with Wayne, another example of Graeham's eye for a replacement.

When the album *First Under The Wire* was released in July 1979, with a picture of the band sitting in the stands at Waverley Football Park, there was a space left between me and Derek, signifying where George would have sat. Beeb reportedly didn't like the cover but it looked great to me, especially when we saw it as a huge billboard on Sunset Boulevard in LA. We thought we'd made the big time when we saw that.

First Under The Wire reached number two in Australia, tying with *Diamantina Cocktail* for highest chart position. It was also our highest charting album in the US, reaching number ten on the Billboard charts. By the end of the year, it would be certified by RIAA for platinum sales of one million with singles, 'Lonesome Loser' and 'Cool Change', both making the US top ten.

I remember David Briggs writing 'Lonesome Loser' when we were rooming together on tour but when he first presented it to the band it wasn't accepted; he had to work on it a bit more before it was recorded by John Boylan. 'Lonesome Loser' begins with an a cappella opening, like our other hits 'Happy Anniversary Baby' and 'It's A Long Way There' and is indicative of the band's signature sound. In 1980, it was also the first of our songs to receive a Grammy nod for Best Vocal Group Performance. Well done, Davo!

My new flirtation with sailing led me to writing the song 'Cool Change', which lyrically reflected my mood at the time: 'Now that my life is so prearranged / I know that it's time for a cool change.' Maybe, I was subconsciously talking to myself. Producer John Boylan and I had to do some serious lobbying with the rest of the band for it to be included on *First Under The Wire* because Graeham and Beeb thought it was 'too personal'.

'What? Of course, it's personal,' I said. 'I wrote it!'

The recording process would frustrate me; it was if songs were beginning to be constructed rather than performed and enjoyed. I once sang a song over and over again for a day and a half before the others were satisfied. It was a good song but one fans would hardly remember. It was a turning point for me.

Graeham ran the show; he was always looking for new equipment, guitars, amplifiers and organising rehearsal time to get that edge and he wanted everything done by the book. He would turn up for rehearsal or a recording, leave and then we wouldn't see him until the next time. He wasn't one to have dinner with us or hang and round and have a drink with the crew, like we did.

On tour, Graeham especially liked to make lists of what he felt was missing in our performances. 'You sang this word instead of that,' he would write on a long list for everyone. We retained a professional respect of each other rather than a close friendship.

Beeb was the buffer between Graeham and me, and the conduit of communication. Don't get me wrong, I enjoyed the good times we had together but what we were doing as a band was hardly going to change the world. I was often known for being 'grumpy' during the recording phase, but I think I was just trying to keep a sense of reality in proceedings.

Birtles and Goble were always pushing their songs, some of which weren't that good, and I was pushing mine but I wasn't as prolific as them so it was a battle for me. In 1979, Birtles and Goble released their album *The Last Romance* which included all the songs rejected by LRB. The project produced a couple of singles, including the extraordinarily sentimental 'I'm Coming Home' which became a hit nowhere but the Philippines! They just weren't LRB songs.

In the second half of the year, I finished a solo session with some Sydney players and released my version of a Bobby Darin song that I'd always liked, 'Dream Lover' which made the Australian top ten. Everyone was branching out and spreading their creative wings; David Briggs had perhaps the biggest success of anyone in LRB when he produced Australian Crawl's debut album, *The Boys Light Up.* I think David had found where he was happiest – in the recording studio.

In 1980, Graeham Goble then agreed to produce John Farnham's 'comeback' album *Uncovered.* I was too busy and too tuned out to notice what was happening. That year would turn out to be one of major changes for me.

While on a Sydney visit, I was on a friend's boat on the harbour and I passed an impressive looking Victorian house with a 'for sale' sign on its foreshore jetty. On the plane back to Melbourne, I found a newspaper left in the seat pocket with a real estate ad for that same house. I used this coincidence to contact the agent as soon as we landed and viewed the property on my next trip to Sydney, which happened to be the following weekend.

Overleaf: Flying high, LRB was a 'stadium' act by the late 1970s and everyone is working hard on stage ... it was a *very* long way there.

I fell in love with the Anchorage as the house was called and armed with brochures and photos convinced Jo that we should move to Sydney and live on the harbour in historic Birchgrove in this four-storey home. Jo was reticent to begin with; being a Melbourne girl with still so many close friends around us at the time, not to mention the LRB headquarters, but I knew we could be happy as Sydneysiders.

We bought it as double block for just under $300,000 which shocked some at the time, especially Mum and Dad, and moved there in the new year leaving our Melbourne home in the safe hands of close friends Barry Bissell and Ernie Rose. Barry was a very well-known radio 'jock' and Ernie, of course, had been a big part of my recording career for many years. By this stage I had swapped our Alfa for a big seven series BMW and we arrived at the Anchorage with our cat, which promptly disappeared up the first chimney it could find.

The Anchorage had been built for a timber merchant sea captain who imported timber from the Pacific in the late 1800s. The 'widow's walk' on the roof was so named because it afforded a 360-degree view of the harbour and his wife would know of his return from voyages with ample time to get rid of lovers! Or so the story went ... it only added to the charm of this elegant, freestanding home on the Balmain peninsula, with a ten-minute ferry ride to Circular Quay. Jo fell for it as I had and put her good taste in interior design to good use.

My Bertram was delivered by truck from Melbourne and swung on its mooring below our 'Victorian skyscraper'. We installed a floating pontoon and began exploring Sydney's waterways. We also did extensive landscaping to the lower garden, which nestled under the sandstone rock overhang, had a pool installed and brought in more rocks from the Blue Mountains to surround it. Life was good and we lived there happily for the next twenty years.

Jo and I had been a couple for five years so it seemed logical that we were compatible and should marry. The wedding had to be in Melbourne and we decided to have it in Dunleavy's in Albert Park, our favourite restaurant, owned and run by our dear friend Don. On another note, playing quietly in the corner on most weekends was Colin Hay in pre-Men At Work solo mode).

On 4 May 1980, about fifty family and friends attended the nuptials. My best man was John Boylan and it was a day of full-on fun and love, or perhaps, lovely fun. The happy newlyweds took off to Rome for a brief honeymoon where it rained most of the time but we enjoyed Italy's hospitality.

Jo and I joined LRB in Hamburg for a European tour before heading back to the US. The band played a large festival in Munich alongside Don McLean, Bob Marley and our old friends Fleetwood Mac. Marley's camp was lost in haze of 'ganga' and the 'Macs' had a tent straight from the film *Camelot* with rows of bunting and flags. Little River Band had two caravans but we managed to steal the show, marred by torrential rain, when the sun appeared exactly at the moment we started our set.

We had a stopover gig and a day off in London, where we sold out the famous Rainbow Theatre in Finsbury. One of our backstage guests that night was John McEnroe, who had met Glenn Wheatley on a flight over from the States. Wimbledon was about to begin (McEnroe was beaten by Björn Borg in the final) and the original 'Superbrat' turned up at the backstage door, yelling to the doorman, 'You can't be serious! Get fucking Wheatley!' Who knew Mac was a such a fan?

Success in England remained tantalising out of reach for LRB. In one review, influential music magazine *Melody Maker* dismissed us as being 'sub-Eagles' and we were often pilloried and pigeon-holed for being 'soft rock'. We closely resembled the Eagles on that score, but they were more organic and incredibly tight as a band. We were also tight but we didn't take enough risks on stage with our music.

We supported the Eagles in the US just before the band split up in July 1980. The first two shows were at the Yale Bowl in front of 70,000 people and then Giants Stadium, New Jersey. Being close to John Boylan, and having begun their early career in LA as members of Linda Ronstadt's then backing band, Glenn Frey and Don Henley were very welcoming to us.

The Eagles threw a great party one night on the thirty-fifth floor of our hotel. Jo was just as thrilled that the actor Michael Douglas was there. The band catered for everyone, with drinks and food on a trolley, along with weed and cocaine. That night I saw David Briggs inhale the end of a joint lying on a bed with the singer Eddie Money; when Davo laughed I swear I saw two sparks come out of his mouth.

I bonded with the other Glenn in the room and we dropped a telephone book from the balcony into the pool below to the huge applause of our guests.

******

Life with LRB was beginning to get hectic for me; exhausting, confusing and repetitive. I was tired of 'stoking the star maker machinery behind the popular song' as Joni Mitchell so eloquently put it. We spent a long time away from home making good money on the road but touring was a haze: college towns, clubs, civic centres, theatres and university halls full of crowds of 2000–3000 people, and wonderful rococo and Art Deco theatres across the states. The tours were becoming routine, as were our performances.

I felt that our song quality was waning too. We needed to refresh as a band and I wanted to take some time off. We had all this money all of a sudden, so let's enjoy it, take a holiday and rejuvenate the band. I couldn't understand the others wanting to keep touring and touring. When LRB finished touring at the end of 1980 I was ready to quit the band if things didn't change and told the guys as much.

Enjoying a day off from touring with members of the LRB road crew at Billy Bob's in Fort Worth, Texas (Ernie Rose is standing left and Peter Rooney is centre, wearing the sombrero). Steve Housden (back left in sombrero) has joined the band so this would be 1981 in the US.

Newly married, I missed my new life with Jo. At the Anchorage, we removed ourselves from band politics and embraced our new life on glamorous Sydney Harbour. Finally, I decided to write the band an open letter. I was taking a huge punt and putting myself on the line. I was expressing myself and my feelings at the time and set myself up for a mighty fall. I began with:

As one who had often been accused (and rightly so) of non-communication and insularity, I thought it was time I should try to communicate the reasons behind my present stand regarding my future with LRB ... Over the last three years I've adopted the position of 'just' being the singer and spokesperson for the band and have largely withdrawn from the policymaking and politicking decisions within the band ... just doing my job, as it were. This stance, of course, has led to my insularity which I admit at this time is a problem to

173

myself and I know to all of you, so now I reluctantly hold the positions of being Grumpy amongst all the dwarfs.

I outlined what I saw as the many successes we had during what we described as phase one of LRB's journey: our coming together as a band, breaking nationally with 'Curiosity (Killed The Cat)' and then, in America, with 'It's A Long Way There'. I also acknowledged the contribution of David Briggs and George McArdle while reminding Graeham, Beeb and Derek of what I still thought was a hasty and ill-advised decision to replace Roger McLachlan.

In phase two of the band's evolution, our live performances had contributed to the respect the band had gained in America. Without blowing my own trumpet, I felt personally gratified by my own work in this area as the front man. However:

> During this time the common ground that swept us through phase one has slowly been replaced by other considerations and motivations that seem to plague successful bands. So much so that at this present time, it is my opinion that personalities and personal monetary ambition is now the driving force with the band and our common ground or platform as professional entertainers/musicians has dwindled to a dangerous low.

How could we continue to play the same repertoire of eighteen songs and retain our integrity, I asked? I was also critical of myself but I believed we were fooling ourselves and the public that everything was fine because of our success. The cracks in the facade were getting wider, however, and we shouldn't underestimate our audience's ability to see it.

I then outlined what we needed to do if we were to go forward:

> Little River Band is full of so much bullshit it needs an enema, if not, major surgery. It's time for a change and not a cool one

174

if we are going to survive and move on to that elusive 'next stage'. I am not advocating complete replacement of individual members but if surgery is to be avoided then an attitude and role adjustment must be made to happen.

My solution was radical. Graeham Goble was a 'square peg in a round hole' on tour and I believed he should retire from performing with the band. No-one could deny his massive contribution to our success but he should concentrate on the areas in which he truly excelled: songwriting, studio production and helping with the policy making decisions in the band. His place on tour could be taken by a percussionist/horn player who could sing, although Wayne Nelson already had Graeham's vocal parts covered on stage.

I finished with:

... Now I feel after giving myself time to think, that unless the change is affected, and I must say again that is vital to the future of LRB, then the change necessary must come from me making my resignation as singer for LRB official.

I don't want this to happen, in fact, I want to do more ... I'm sure you all do too, but the necessary course adjustment has to be made so that we can all put our personalities aside and let our talents, collectively, do the job.

Don't hesitate to approach me about anything you feel you want to discuss with me.

Sincerely Glenn

If the other members of the band took my suggestions on board, I never knew. No-one ever spoke with me about it. LRB would struggle on for another year before the situation came to a head.

CHAPTER 14

Villain of the Peace

If you were to drill a hole from Melbourne through the centre of the earth and out the other side of the world, you would come close to landing on the island of Montserrat, of the Leeward group of islands in the Caribbean, as far as you can possibly get from Oz. To reach there by air in the early 1980s took about forty-two hours but it's a little slice of heaven.

In 1981, LRB and John Boylan mutually decided that a change of producer was needed after four albums together. Different names were put forward by the record company before George Martin was mentioned. The Beatles' George Martin.

We were all over the moon at that possibility. George Martin wants to produce us? Really?

George owned AIR (Associated Independent Recording) Studios in Montserrat. Paul McCartney had just vacated the premises, having recorded his new album *Tug Of War* there. Paul McCartney and Stevie Wonder had recorded 'Ebony And Ivory' together weeks before we arrived, so we felt good to be in their company so to speak.

Exhausted, but excited, we arrived in Montserrat in early 1981 via LA, Miami and Antigua and were met at AIR Studios by George and his large German shepherd Bosun. Jo took a while to relax around the dog, having been attacked by a similar dog as a child. Bosun, however, would only lick you to death.

The island is 18 kilometres long and 11 wide and the studio

An alternate shot of my photoshoot for my solo album *Villain of the Peace* by Geoff Hales. Standing on Hollywood Boulevard not far from the famous Frederick's lingerie establishment. (Courtesy Geoff Hales)

is almost dead centre, high above the blue Caribbean Sea. The studio was roomy and modern, with an adjoining dining room and a beautiful pool and terrace looking down across a lush lawn to the sea. Accommodation was in three attractive serviced villas, housing ten people.

The setting was perfect to produce some good music but things were not so rosy within the band. Beeb and Graeham lobbied hard for their material and had little confidence in my songwriting input by this stage. I put forward a song called 'Man On Your Mind', which had largely been written by Kerryn Tolhurst from the Dingoes. He had come to me with it partially finished, needing some help with some of the lyrics and middle eight, which I gladly provided. There's a line at the end of the song that goes, 'You can't change your life by changing your name.' I was writing about getting married, how changing your last name doesn't change your life. Graeham was into numerology and added an 'e' to his name, and somehow thought it was about him. The song was initially rejected.

I wrote a letter to George Martin and the band, putting forward my case, and my song was reconsidered. George had to use all his charm and diplomacy to keep on top of our 'politics' ... the Beatles were a cakewalk compared to LRB, George told Wheatley one day.

I got on really well with George Martin and will always look back on working with him as a career highlight. Just getting to know him on personal level was a great experience and it wasn't hard to get him talking about our heroes, the Beatles. George shared lots of recording anecdotes with us about 'the boys' during our time there. I also knew all the words to his comedy records with the Goons and Peter Sellers, which was a plus.

Unfortunately, David Briggs fell out with George over one of the songs we were recording. George told David how the song should be played and David didn't handle it well at all. The

With the wonderful George Martin recording *Time Exposure* in Monserrat in 1981. The island was decimated by Hurricane Hugo at the end of the decade and the recording studios abandoned but working with Sir George was one of the great highlights of my career.

178

situation festered, David took himself off and didn't mix with the rest of the band for days on end.

Wayne Nelson, on the other hand, proved to be a great band member and we got on really well. He called me the Colonel and he was really a nice guy. Wayne changed the dynamic of LRB once again. He was also an accomplished singer and he rounded out our sound.

Graeham liked his voice and started to tailor his songs to suit Wayne. He wanted Wayne to sing lead in two of his songs, 'Nights Owls' and 'Take It Easy On Me'. I drew the line at Wayne singing two songs. 'I'm the singer in the band,' I said. 'Let me do a version of each and you could choose the best one.' Wayne sang 'Nights Owls' and while I took the lead on 'Take It Easy On Me', he handled the bridge which was too high for me.

It was a real challenge. Beeb and Graeham had sung leads on album tracks before but this was not so much a case of me

protecting my turf, so to speak, but I had to have something to do on stage. I was the lead singer! I wasn't angry but I just kept my wits about me and remembered the band's 'revolving door'.

Sometimes Jo and I would go down to Agouti, a bar with live reggae and rum to escape the tension. Viv Richards was the 'master blaster' in the cricket world at the time and a hero of the Caribbean so I talked a lot of cricket with the locals. We spent six wonderful weeks there recording *Time Exposure* but for me, unfortunately, the experience was somewhat spoilt by the squabbling in the band.

Working with George Martin didn't help the band in the end, nor did it paper over the cracks in the group that were starting to get wider and wider. We finished the album and George took it back to England to mix. Unfortunately, Graeham and Beeb disliked the finished product so much they decided to remix it themselves back in Melbourne with Ernie Rose, without telling George. Understandably, George was very upset and wanted to take his name off the album but that would have defeated the purpose of him producing it in the first place. Thankfully, the record company talked George into leaving it on. The whole thing was embarrassing and I was especially embarrassed for George.

Time Exposure didn't turn everyone on, although 'Night Owls' and 'Man On Your Mind' were both hit singles. The latter song, which was originally rejected by the band, was to be the last top-ten we had with that line-up. The album reached number nine in Australia, and number twenty-one in the US, and was eventually certified gold by RIAA.

After our Monserrat experience, we all felt that David Briggs was out of line; he was too angry, too moody and using too much dope. David and I had become firm friends over the years and his work ethic was admirable but his cannabis intake was formidable and that hastened his departure from LRB. David remains a very respected mastering engineer and still plays a mean guitar. We still see each other from time to time.

By the time the album *Time Exposure* appeared, Stephen Housden, a migrant like myself and a unique guitar player (ex-Stevie Wright Band, The Imports) in his own right had replaced David as our lead guitarist. We toured extensively over the next year to promote the album but internal tensions within the band only got worse.

LRB were on a treadmill; I wanted to include other people's songs, expand the horizons a bit more rather than the philosophy of the more we tour the more money we make. I was looking for that ease on stage that other bands had and to change the dynamics a little, but we were too neat and precise for that; everything had to be in its place. I tried to walk away from it because I got angry too easily, which didn't do anyone any good, so I just stopped communicating.

'Cool Change,' singing harmony with Beeb Birtles.

As 1982 rolled around, I made it clear to the other members of the group that we should take a break from touring and re-energise. Too many groups run out of steam on the road and their creativity suffers because they don't have the necessary stamina and energy. That was LRB ...

In February, I was summoned down to Melbourne for a meeting with Graeham and Beeb in Glenn Wheatley's office for what I though a routine 'think tank' about touring again. I told them how I felt and that they had to make the decision. They said they already had. A vote had been taken, I was told, and I was being replaced by John Farnham.

What?

Wayne and Steve apparently supported me but the Birtles, Goble, Pellicci group won out. I couldn't believe I had become the scapegoat for all our problems and was the next in a long line of revolving door membership changes.

I phoned Jo, who was back home in Sydney, and told her the news. Jo got upset because well, she's my wife, and a very emotional person. Look out! The previous year, Beeb Birtles had written to Jo and I and told us that he would support me no matter what. Beeb got the teary call from Jo, 'How could you?' He later wrote in his autobiography that he immediately regretted how it had all played out and his own relationship with Glenn Wheatley and John Farnham wouldn't last the distance.

Looking back, at the time it must have appeared to Graeham Goble that all the stars were aligning. The previous year, he had produced John Farnham's album and he obviously felt there was something in his voice he could write for. Graeham wrote or co-wrote nine of the ten songs on the album, all except John's version of the Lennon and McCartney song 'Help!', and the players on that album were like the who's who of LRB – Goble, David Briggs, Derek Pellicci, Wayne Nelson and even Barry Sullivan played bass on one track. Graeham may not agree, but I think the decision was already made in

Me, Beeb and Graeham on stage ... it looks like I am changing a lightbulb mid-concert. 'Flares 'R' Us', it *must* be the 1970s.

his mind – he wanted John Farnham in LRB at my expense.

Was it also convenient for Glenn Wheatley for John Farnham to join the band? Glenn was managing Farnham at the time and had co-produced the *Uncovered* album. Glenn has gone to some length in the media to say he did not put John forward as my replacement for LRB. I have gathered enough information over the years that Glenn didn't want me to leave LRB, but he didn't stick up for me either. LRB made it clear to him that they would go with another management company if he didn't agree. Glenn should have stood his ground and said no.

Looking back on it now, and if I'm being honest with myself, if Glenn Wheatley hadn't kicked down the door to the US, I don't think I would have continued much longer with LRB. Don't get me wrong; I was happy with our music but I just didn't feel the same fellowship with the group that I had with Axiom and certainly the Twilights. But the door was open to America, the Holy Grail, and any misgivings I may have had at the time were overshadowed by our success there.

After seven years with LRB, I was out of the band. I was pissed off because I thought they were all making a big mistake. I was hurt, angry, vindictive even, but I told myself it was just another band and it wasn't the end of the world. My time in the Twilights, Axiom and Esperanto had each come to an end. This was no different.

That night I found sympathy with Brian Cadd and Johnny Walker! Then I picked myself up and got on with it.

As the dust settled and the empty bottles were discarded, my 'fuck you' attitude took over. I finished some songs inspired by recent events and went back to LA to record a solo album. That's what drove me to put my solo album out so quickly. In retrospect, I should have moved to America and met with John Boylan and my record company and then worked out a clear strategy so I could find my feet as a solo artist.

I moved in with John Boylan at Nichols Canyon and we

began pre-production in early 1982. We recorded backing tracks in the famous Sound City studios, in Van Nuys, before finishing off at the record plant in LA. Such was John's profile, and mine through LRB, that it allowed us to use some great musicians on that album: Andrew Gold (Linda Ronstadt Band), Bill Payne (Little Feat), Mike Botts (Bread) and Bob Glaud (Jackson Browne) formed a great backing band with guest stars including Randy Meisner, Eagles' Timothy B Schmit and Don Felder, Jeff Baxter (Steely Dan and Doobie Brothers), Garth Hudson (The Band), Tom Scott (Blues Brothers), Waddy Wachtel, Michael Boddicker and David Linley, while my friends Brian Cadd, Sharon O'Neill and Wendy Matthews also joined in enthusiastically.

Canadian singer Wendy Matthews came to the session on the arm of Geoff Hales, my old friend from London who travelled to Paris with me and Gael McKay on an infamous weekend trip in the 1970s. We became firm friends and when we learned that she was a singer, we used her on the album. She later came to Australia as part of the touring band for the album and we still enjoy our friendship to this day.

Garth Hudson, the keyboard player for the Band, came into the studio to play accordion on the track 'Martinique', which was written by John Boylan. Garth was a totally unassuming guy who embraced me warmly at the end of the session and thanked us for the gig before driving off into the night. He had the unfortunate habit of humming along with his playing, which was picked up by the nearest microphone. John and I would be hiding behind the recording console looking at each other. How do you tell a legendary musician he's stuffing up the take?

I reluctantly brought up the subject with him. 'Excuse me Garth? You're mumbling along with the playing.'

'Am I? Oh yeah, I do that sometimes ...' We did another couple of takes and he did it every time. In the end we had to put the microphone on the floor.

The album was titled *Villain Of The Peace*, a play on words that

reflected how I saw myself in LRB, and was released in August 1982. I was very excited to have recorded what I thought was a strong collection of songs with such great musicians and eagerly awaited the reaction to it. It was received somewhat 'quietly' and just as quietly faded into the distance. It got little airplay, even in Australia, although a single 'Rock 'n' Roll Soldier' reached the top forty. It was the biggest disappointment of my career.

It's funny but many people have told me that they loved that album and I'm proud of it. 'Angry Words', a tune penned by Brian Cadd, is my pick on the album and I always liked 'Will You Stand With Me'. 'A Cry In The Jungle Bar', a song I wrote with John Boylan, is another favourite with great guitar from Jeff 'Skunk' Baxter. Maybe we should have paid more attention to the other songs on the album – a cover of 'Summer In The City'? The songs just didn't gel.

I toured the album in Australia with what I cynically called 'The Should've Known Better Band', which included Wendy Matthews who was soon to make Australia her home (she later had a hit with 'The Day You Went Away' in 1992). The tour was not well subscribed but it was a crowded dance card as far Australian bands were concerned at that time. I should have taken my own advice and gone off and recharged my batteries.

As they say in the business, excrement occurs!

******

The Little River Band's music is often described as 'middle of the road' or 'MOR', although I think we rose to the occasion in other genres more times than people gave us credit for. MOR is not such a bad place to be; LRB found an audience waiting for us there and we had our greatest success there.

And if you could apply MOR to your life in a philosophical way, I would happily place myself there too. I've often described myself as 'philosophical driftwood'. I'll wash up on a beach somewhere and have a look around, learn a bit more and then float around again for a while until I find the next landfall. I know that sounds a bit naive but it works for me – take a pinch of this add a little bit of that and see if it tastes good.

Rock god (or is it cod?). Did I leave my wallet in the dressing room?

It is said that one of the things that sets us apart from the other species is the ability to make choices. Well, we certainly have a lot to choose from in this crowded world today. For example, what sort of music do you like? Back when I was growing up you had three: pop-rock, jazz or classical. Now you can go into a huge depository on your music 'devices' and pick countless subgenres in each of the above categories. By the time I've made may choice my interest has gone.

There are just so many music doors to open and paths to follow or not follow. I've been down a few in my time but I know where I want to be. And it's not about the fame either. You see, if you overemphasise celebrity you won't hear the creativity. As my song 'Will You Stand With Me' says:

The singer's song will not be heard
If the applause is much too loud.

Music is a many-faceted and beautifully cut diamond, the light shining in many directions. Art is in the eye of the beholder ... and the ear of listener.

I now realise that life is a broad spectrum of colour, the edges of which may be black and white, but the colours in between are beautiful and varied. Charting the middle path in life is much harder because of the many choices presented to you along the way ... decisions, decisions! Black or white? Good or bad? Yin or yang, and so on. In the end, it's up to you; it's your choice to make. That's when the living begins ... and the trouble starts!

It seems to me if you go out to the edges it can be a very dangerous way to live your life but you don't have to make as many choices in life. You just surrender to a dogma or creed, or let your vices take over ... drugs, drink, material possessions, fame.

In the 1960s when I was starting out, the youth culture was just coming of age. We were living the flower-power dream, 'Love Is All You Need'; and both mysticism and drugs were being investigated with equal gusto. It took me a long time to know where the line was and if I was crossing it.

I had tried marijuana and was interested in LSD. Terry Britten shared my curiosity too, and he and Peter Brideoake 'tripped' occasionally, as did I, briefly. When I was on a US tour with LRB, I thought there was nothing better than relaxing after a gig by going back to our hotel room and watching *Saturday Night Live* with a red wine in one hand and smoking a joint. Cocaine was a much more insidious drug because people could hide their usage and still function to a certain degree, although abuse of any drug can make the gentlest soul psychotic. Heroin was for junkies.

The only person I know who was able to function creatively while high on drugs was the (late) celebrated Australian artist Brett Whitely. I, like many others, was in awe of his talent. Funnily enough, he liked to play the Little River Band when he painted.

Organised religions hold little interest for me and fundamentalism definitely doesn't either. I haven't practised any organised religion as such but if I was to make a choice I am swayed towards Buddhism.

My interest in all things cosmic or mystic came also from the writings of Paul Brunton, especially *Search In Secret India* and the sequel *Search In Secret Egypt*, reinforced by my visit to the pyramids in 1965. Indeed, the centre piece of *Secret Egypt* is his account of a night spent in the same King's Chamber in which I lingered briefly.

I was introduced to Transcendental Meditation by way of the Beatles, more specifically through George Harrison and his interest in Indian music and culture, and find that relaxing as well. Meditation has been a part of my life for years now with lots of 'gaps' along the way filled with that old black magic ... hedonism! That moment of bliss has largely eluded me, despite my best efforts.

I no longer rigidly stick to regular 'sittings' but still use the technique to ease my way through life. But as I have learnt, there are so many paths up the mountain.

CHAPTER 15

Back in LRB

The 1980s had begun with recording with George Martin in Monserrat, but the decade turned into a somewhat confusing time, with many opportunities opening up for me after my departure from LRB. At age thirty-seven, and after twenty years in the music business, I felt I had something to prove, so after my solo album was released, I teamed up with Renée Geyer and released a cover of the old Dusty Springfield song 'Goin' Back' on Mushroom Records in February 1983.

I took my love of sailing and the freedom I find on the ocean to a new level when I became involved with Australia's America's Cup campaign. Former Seeker Bruce Woodley penned a motivational song called, 'We're Coming To Get You' and asked me to sing it. It was quite stirring and singing it introduced me into the challenger team, bankrolled by Melbourne billionaire Richard Pratt.

However, Alan Bond's *Australia II* campaign won the honour of contesting the series against Dennis Connor's *Liberty* and I was offered the job of hosting a documentary filmed in Newport, Rhode Island, where the Cup was to be defended by the New York Yacht Club. I moved in with the film crew into a Cape Cod-style house for a month as the two crews prepared to battle the five-race competition. Hopes were high that we could finally wrest the cup from the holders after 132 years, the longest tenure in sporting history. Our hopes rested on the revolutionary

In my more hirsute days ... I don't remember having that much chest hair back in the 1980s. I was much more confident about going back into LRB the second time around after my solo years.

winged keel on our boat designed by Ben Lexcen, skippered by John Bertrand and hyped by Alan Bond, the self-made magnate from Western Australia.

I had little to do for the first weeks as the race was often interrupted by light seas or lack of wind. I ingratiated myself with the crew of *Australia II* and helped myself to the refreshments designated for the Aussies at the local bar. Men At Work had a hit with 'Down Under' and it eclipsed my offering and became the real anthem of the team, and deservedly so.

The drama played out beautifully, with Dennis Conner stretching *Liberty* to a 3–1 lead and things looked ominous. The script was being written out daily on the course but my contribution to the documentary could not be filmed until the result had been decided. Months before, I had been booked to sing the national anthem at the Australian Rules grand final at the MCG so I had to fly home from the East Coast of the US to Melbourne, leaving the race result in precarious limbo.

To complicate things even further I had a lung infection, probably from enjoying myself too much, but flew the twenty-four hours back to Melbourne and arrived the day before the 'bounce' between the Hawks and the Bombers. I managed to stand up and deliver 'Advance Australia Fair' live with a military brass band echoing around the 'G', and a chest infection to boot!

Jo and I watched the first quarter and then flew straight back

The lovely Renée Geyer had a reputation for being somewhat of a diva but she's a good woman and our 1983 collaboration *Goin' Back* is one of the best live recording I've ever done.

Singer Wendy Matthews has become a great friend, and a close confidante of my wife Jo's over the years, since coming to Australia in support of my solo album *Villain Of The Peace*. Here we are together when I was surprised by the *This Is Your Life* team in 2004.

to Newport, Rhode Island. During the epic, seventy-two hour journey *Australia II* had fought back to level the score to 3–all and we arrived back on the morning of the deciding race. We rushed to our filming boat on the course just as the race began. *Liberty* gained the ascendancy and at the last mark it looked to be all over. We were so exhausted, we excused ourselves and went below for a nap and waited for the inevitable.

I was shaken awake to cries of 'Get up, we're in front'. Needless to say, at 5.21 pm on 26 September 1983, *Australia II* crossed the line in front of *Liberty* to win the America's Cup, four races to three and grasped the 'Auld Mug' after 132 years. Bedlam ensued, and the next twenty-four hours were a daze but I certainly will never forget the sight of Alan Bond at the dock that night, revealing the boat's secret keel to the world.

I completed my part in what became the documentary *Aussie Assault* and went home to rest, having enjoyed the gig of a lifetime and been paid for it too. We also made some great new friends and I was later invited to sing at Sue Bond's wedding, which was a hoot in itself. The reception was held at Eileen and Alan's waterfront mansion in Perth and my band and I were winched from the middle of the Swan River to meet the guests on a wharf to do my 'bit'. Strangely, someone had miscalculated the height of the tide and as I began 'Dream Lover' my stage was three feet below the dance floor, which subsequently collapsed into a dish of revellers! Champagne flowed all night and on to breakfast. Yo, ho, ho and a bottle of Krug!

In 1984, I tried my hand as a breakfast radio jock on a newly branded Magic 11, the former Sydney juggernaut 2UW. I was asked to do three months with co-host Ron E Sparks, with the wonderful Tim Webster reading news and sport, and ended up doing five months. I put up with 4 am wake-up calls and working three hours on air (6 am to 9 am) five days a week before accepting defeat. It was just too hard doing shows at night and getting up in the morning.

In 1986, the ABC contacted me to host a show for television called *Rock Video*. A year before MTV launched in Australia, it was one of the first video-clip shows on TV and I got to interview some great people, including Led Zeppelin's Robert Plant.

I had come up with an idea for an indie-style revue show based on my taste in music, incorporating some satirical impersonations. I had always liked taking the mickey and, as luck would have it, Jo and I bumped into actor-producer Graeme Blundell in the street one day and Jo told him of our plans. He had just been made the creative director for Kinselas, a nightclub, restaurant and theatre in Oxford Street in Darlinghurst. Would I like to collaborate with him to co-produce a show?

My idea had been reinforced by running into the Eddies, a rockabilly outfit of aficionados of the early rock 'n' roll years. I'd sat in with them from time to time and had lots of fun revisiting that genre again by bringing them on board as the backing band for the show. We needed two girls in the show and auditioned and hired Dannielle Gaha and Jodie Gillies, two fabulous talents full of nonstop energy.

We all pitched in and with help from writer Bob Hudson, we came up with *One For The Money*, the first lines of 'Blue Suede Shoes', as the title for a series of shows based on the early days of rock. We paid homage to the good, the bad, and the kitsch!

On stage with the complete cast of our review *One For The Money* at Kinsela's in 1986. The band were the wonderful Eddies and our backup singers (at back from left) were the lovely and talented Jodie Gillies and Dannielle Gaha.

195

We had nine performers who loved what they were doing and we had a hit show right off the bat.

The show revolved around me doing various impersonations of JO'K, Elvis, Buddy Holly, Little Richard, ABBA and Tina Turner – in full drag I might add! The show ran for six sold-out weeks and was a must-see for fans of unpretentious theatre and music. We also toured it in Adelaide, Brisbane, Perth and Melbourne. The show kept us busy for the next two or three years doing on-demand extra seasons. We followed this with *Two For The Show* (1988–89) and *Go Cat Go* (1990–91).

We broke box office records for a great theatre in Perth called the Regal. The Eddies really did swing, just like the music dictated, and with Jody and Danielle taking the lead they were hilarious doing Abba and *Brady Bunch* send-ups. Our shows put Kinselas back on the map as a great place for fun and food. The restaurant was run by Tony Bilson and working in his kitchen was Tetsuya Wakuda; both were to become the doyens of the Sydney gastronomic scene. Thirty years later I'm still being asked, 'Are you doing Tina Turner tonight?' You can't beat a man dressed up as a woman for top-class entertainment!

I also acted in a couple of musicals during this time. I was asked to join a touring company in the roles of Dr Scott and Eddie in *The Rocky Horror Show*. Russell Morris played Riff Raff and we toured from Cairns to Brisbane, having spent two weeks rehearsing in Townsville. I enjoyed the cast and fellowship but found the show itself to be quite puerile. I travelled a lot with the show's promoter in his Fairlane and one morning woke up in the passenger seat, next to him, doing 60 kilometres an hour through a cane field north of Mackay, exiting back onto the highway to oncoming traffic. My driver had also fallen asleep!

'Glenny Rogers' anyone? I loved rushing off the stage and hurriedly getting dressed for the next act during my review shows. I was a show-off and it really appealed to my 'theatrical' bent that harks back to my Twilights days. Open the fridge and I'll do twenty minutes for you.

As the decade closed, in 1989 I accepted an offer to join the production of *Evita* in the role of Che Guevara at the State Theatre in Sydney. I enjoy the ensemble work of the theatre; it's a different discipline to being in a band and has that feeling of 'legitimate' show business; not that it means the music industry is illegitimate, although I have been called a bastard a couple of times! *Evita* starts and ends with a funeral, which seemed to disturb some of the blue-haired patrons at the matinée performances, but I relished the role of one of the most famous contemporary revolutionaries and had great song to sing as well, 'High Flying, Adored'.

Che's beret covered my fast disappearing hair for the duration of the show but the voice of Irving Azoff was ringing in my ears. Azoff, the Eagles' manager and the then A&R vice-president with MCM Records, was interested in reviving the Little River Band. He was quoted as saying, 'Get that Shorrock guy back in the band, put a rug on him and we can make some hits again.'

I was fitted with my 'rug', constructed by a master craftsman for $1500 and paid for by MCA. Everyone told me it looked great but Jo hated it and it spent its final years hiding in the back of my undies drawer!

******

In 1986, I heard on the grapevine that John Farnham was not happy being in LRB and had left the band. Glenn Wheatley was branching out into management of sports stars and had plans for John as a solo artist again. When Geoffrey Schuhkraft took over the management reins of LRB, they approached me about coming back to the band. Surprisingly, Graeham Goble thought it was a good idea too. Never say never.

So, with the knowledge that John Boylan would produce our next album, I agreed to navigate the waters of the Little River Band once again. Geoffrey Schuhkraft had formed a partnership

with Paul Palmer, who had managed Player, a band we had toured with years earlier. He hooked me up with two ex-members of Player to write with and I contributed three songs on the *Monsoon* album, which was recorded at AAV (Melbourne) and finished at the famous Capitol Studios in LA in 1988. Ken Done whipped up a suitable cover and we relaunched LRB with 'Love Is A Bridge', a nice single from Goble and Housden, which got the 'River' flowing again. Having Irving Azoff as our champion at MCA was a big plus but we were shocked to hear that he had left the company just as our album was released. It was a huge letdown and although the single did well, the resulting album did not set the world on fire. We toured successfully but the end of the Farnham years had stopped band momentum in its tracks so our high hopes were somewhat dented.

That year, we invited the Eagles' Glenn Frey to join us on an Australasian tour. He had just released his third solo album,

Soul Searchin' and was keen to return to Australia to promote it. He was billed as our special guest and joined us on stage where he and I took lead vocals on some classic Eagles songs and then he continued on his own with a horn section. Glenn and I had bonded on the road in the US and now we enjoyed singing together.

The highlight of the tour was playing in front of tens of thousands of people on Brisbane's Southbank as part of the Expo 88 Festival, which was recorded on DVD for posterity. Sadly, Glenn passed away suddenly in 2016 and it still brings a lump to my throat watching him and I do 'Take It Easy' and 'Peaceful Easy Feeling' that lovely night. On the strength of that tour's success, we asked Christopher Cross ('Ride Like The Wind', 'Sailing' and 'Arthur's Song') to join us in 1989 for a Hilton Hotel tour.

In 1990, Paul Palmer and MCA put us in the studio with producer Dennis Lambert and we recorded a last-ditch album in his Sherman Oakes home studio in LA. My contribution was the song 'I Dream Alone', with lyrics by Derek Pellicci, but I had little confidence of success this time, although I thought the title song 'Get Lucky' was the most commercial song we had recorded in a long time. The album came out with little fanfare.

LRB integrated singer-songwriter Warren Zevon into our next tour of Australia. Warren was a quirky guy and was a little too radical to fit with our style although his iconic songs went down well with our audiences. My wife Jo and his then girlfriend, Eleanor Mondale, the daughter of former US Vice President Walter Mondale, became great friends. Eleanor was a classic 'sassy broad' who everyone loved.

When we began the US leg of the tour, Graeham decided to leave the band and rest on his laurels. His place was taken by Tony Sciuto, a keyboard player from Baltimore. The line-up of Little River Band was now me, Derek Pellicci, Wayne Nelson, Steve Housden, drummer Peter Beckett and Tony Sciuto. Interestingly,

Back in LRB and receiving gold discs for out 1988 album *Monsoon* from MCA execs. Our then managers of LRB Mark II, Bob Palmer and Geoffrey Schuhkraft, are standing at back between Graeham and Steve.

not one member of this incarnation was a homegrown Australian – LRB comprised four Brits and two Yanks – but it was a happy band and we enjoyed some great live gigs.

LRB were moving into new territory as a 'classic' touring band rather than recording artists. Fans were no longer buying our records but, a little bit older and greyer than in the 1970s, they were still coming to our concerts. I enjoyed my time in this new incarnation of the band, but it wasn't like the old days. The ground had shifted from underneath us.

The north-west states of the US and Alaska were strong regions for LRB and fans always warmly welcomed us. I requested a window seat on the right side whenever we travelled there by plane. On one trip I was treated to a spectacular view of Mount St Helen soon after the eruption in 1980, the devastation both awe inspiring and humbling. We had played Anchorage a couple of times in the past and this time we went further north to Fairbanks, in the backwoods, on the way passing over Mount McKinley (now Denali), America's highest peak.

The weather in Fairbanks Alaska was sunny during the day but temperatures plummeted at night. My room in our basic hotel was below ground, except for a small window high up on the wall. I tried to open it a little for fresh air but managed to break the glass. It was past midnight and they had no night staff on so I spent the night dressed in everything I could wear to keep from freezing.

Another time we played in Juneau, the capital of Alaska, down on the coast of the North Pacific and visited often by cruise ships on their way up the coast from Vancouver, Canada. We were able to see a magnificent nearby glacier and witnessed 'calving' of small icebergs from our position on the water. I've probably seen more of the United States than most Americans.

One other event was also significant but for a very different reason. We had just finished a short run of Europe in 1992, having crossed into East Germany for one performance following the fall of the Berlin Wall, and we were in London for a couple of nights looking forward to a break. Wayne Nelson, our bass player, was meeting his wife Lynette for a holiday in England at Heathrow the next morning. During the night I was woken by someone screaming in obvious distress. It was Wayne. His wife Lynette had driven up from San Diego where they lived, followed by their son Bradley and daughter Aubrey in a neighbour's car, to see her off at LAX Airport. On the way back and almost home, the car was T-boned and Aubrey was thrown from the car and killed instantly.

Wayne had been given this devastating news over the phone and was in a bad way but now had to go to Heathrow and meet his wife, who had no idea what had happened. I could not fathom a worse scenario. It was a shocking time for all involved. When American Airlines learnt of this tragedy, a private area was made available for him to break the news to Lynette and then first-class seats were set aside for them to fly straight back to California on the next flight. Aubrey was just thirteen years old and a beautiful child.

I will never forget the sound that woke me that night. Wayne managed to re-join us months later but things were never the same in the band again. Wayne had no interest in making music and Hal Tupuea, a jolly Maori, took his place for LRB's New Zealand tour in 1993. We also decided to take a break after that trauma.

Wayne and I shared a close friendship, which has unfortunately suffered over the years, but that is somewhat understandable given that he is still playing with LRB.

Overleaf: Two Glenns on stage – working with former Eagles' frontman Glenn Frey at Brisbane Expo in 1988. Sadly missed today, our friendship was caught in the moment when we looked at each other on stage and sang the line from the classic 'Take It Easy': 'We may lose and we may win, though we will never be here again.' It's a touching photograph.

CHAPTER 16

Blazing Salads

On 25 March 1991, I was inducted into the Australian Recording Industry Association (ARIA) Hall of Fame as a solo performer, alongside my contemporary Billy Thorpe, bass-baritone Peter Dawson and jazz musician Don Burrows. Producer Ted Albert, who had sadly passed away the previous November at the young age of forty-three, was posthumously awarded a Life Achievement Award for his work with Albert Studios and the Easybeats, Vanda and Young, and AC/DC.

Hosted by Bob Geldof, the awards were not televised that year and ran for more than three hours. My good friend Wendy Matthews picked up a couple of gongs and John Farnham won best male artist and highest-selling album of the year. It was great to be inducted for my solo work, more than twenty-five years after starting out with the Twilights in the mid-1960s. I now have two Life Achievement Awards and, who knows, maybe the Twilights and Axiom will be inducted in the future and I'll have four!

By the way, I think it's pertinent to point out that I have never received an invitation to the awards except to receive them. One would think the past recipients would automatically be there to show off the industry's legacy.

At that time, I was spending a lot of time at our island home in Fiji. Wakaya Island is part of a huge caldera of an ancient volcano. Eight kilometres long and a more than a kilometre-wide running north to south, on its leeward side are steep cliffs down

Brian Cadd and yours truly in Fiji in the early 1990s – 'The Elderly Brothers'. These songwriting sessions became the basis of our Blazing Salads collaboration during the decade.

to a reef. The windward side slopes down into a large lagoon. The block we fell in love with sits near the highest point of the ridge, looking down to the turquoise sea 150 metres below and faces glorious sunsets.

Some years before, our good friends Judy and Lionel Hunt, Jo's ex-boss from the Campaign Palace, had moved into a house down the road from the Anchorage. The Shorrock and Hunts, joined by Glenn and Gaynor Wheatley, went on a two-week cruise through the Fiji Islands on board a chartered motor-yacht called the *Molly Dean* with a crew of three and four-year-old James Hunt. It was a wonderful South Seas holiday.

Skipper Greg Lawler took us to a small island called Wakaya where a friend of his was managing a company resort. Rob and Lynda Miller lived amongst a hundred or so islanders in a lifestyle I'd often dreamt about. We took a tour of the island with Rob and, on continuation of our cruise, learnt that private blocks of land were for sale. Lionel and I discussed the idea of making an

Our home Kele Kele in Fiji, the circular living space in the middle of the house.

With the lovely Finau, our housekeeper in Fiji during the 1990s. We watched her children grow and had the pleasure of bringing her to Australia over the years.

offer on one. As we fished and dived our way back to Nadi, we called into Wakaya again and walked on a probable site of our new island home.

The company whose resort it was owned and maintained the island with a staff of around 150 villagers and had permission to sell blocks of three acres or more to freehold owners. The lot we chose was owned by a doctor in Finland, who bought it sight unseen, and we were able to buy it from him. There were only four or five houses on the island at the time and we contacted Suva architect Stuart Huggett, who had already built there. We listened to Stuart describe the type of house that was suitable and we said no thanks – this is what we want! We showed him an *Architectural Digest* magazine featuring a house in Central America with circular concrete walls and thatched-roofed pavilions set, resort style, on the naturally terraced block with two circular bedrooms either side of a pool.

He told us how difficult it would be to get a builder to do it that way, with all the materials and workers needing to be barged across from the main island of Viti Levu. We gradually convinced him to take it on and got him excited about our romantic house

brief. Stuart and family became close friends and Kele Kele, as the house became known – 'anchor' in Fijian – became our 'go-to' respite. We were witnesses to the Wakaya Club evolving into a six-star resort with guests including Bill Gates, Tom Cruise, Nicole Kidman and Keith Richards to name but a few. The exclusiveness of the club became more and more difficult to handle, however, and we sold up in the mid-nineties.

However, we drank, dined, dived, sailed and fished for sixteen wonderful years. *Vinaka vaka levu!* (thank you very much).

My fiftieth birthday was celebrated at Kele Kele in 1994 with family and friends in attendance. People of a similar age to me were now heading the business and corporate world and had grown up with my music over the years, so lucrative 'corporate gigs' came my way in the latter half of the decade. I travelled far and wide with my band – Stewart Wilkinson on keyboard and guitar, Pip Joyce on lead guitar, Jason Vorher on bass and Dave Beck on drums, sometimes augmented by Gary Sound on lead guitar. We have had many years on the road and they have presented my music with aplomb ... and custard!

In 1993, on a sabbatical from LRB, I caught up with my old friend and colleague Brian Cadd, who was visiting Oz to attend to some family matters and making music on the Gold Coast with a local band there. I joined him for a week of fun and games, and encouraged by Brian Harris, an old EMI mate of ours, we began thinking about a musical collaboration.

I invited Brian to Fiji for a working holiday and told him to bring his A-Grade songwriting game. We travelled to Kele Kele and started work on songs for an album, one of which was 'When the Words Come' about the tragic loss of Wayne Nelson's daughter, which was still fresh in my mind. We also revisited the Axiom classic 'A Little Ray Of Sunshine', trying to improve on my vocal from more than twenty years before.

Writing songs with Brian Cadd (note the pen in my hand) in Fiji. Brian looks well, 'happy and emotional' after a hard day's work and copious amounts of Côtes du Rhône wine ... blazing salads indeed.

The entrance into
our home in Fiji,
the gardens and
pathway designed
by my wife Jo.

Jo also invited Eleanor Mondale to Fiji, the pair having become close during the Warren Zevon tour. It was an idyllic setting enjoyed by everyone; Eleanor, having broken up with Warren, had a dalliance with the best-looking Fijian in the village below us, inspiring a song we called '(The angel of the fjord and the boy from) Capricorn'. Sadly, she was to pass away from brain cancer in 2011, tragically young at age fifty-one. Her former beau Warren Zevon predeceased her in 2003, age fifty-six.

Following one of the famous chicken curries prepared by our dear housekeeper Finau and lashings of red wine, we were giggling beneath the stars talking about Mel Brooks' films. Brian remarked that his favourite film was 'Blazing Salads' (*Blazing Saddles*) and I instantly said that should be our name this time around.

Upon returning to Australia, we met with EMI and signed a deal. Cadd slept in the attic room of the Anchorage, four floors up, which he aptly named the '*Pant*house'. He returned to Tennessee

to his wife Lynda and their two young kids, Nick and Jessica, in a town south of Nashville called Franklyn, on the Mason–Dixon Line, to prepare his home studio. Jo and I arrived soon after and we spent about a month there working and exploring the Civil War sites around the area. Brian had enlisted a lot of his friends to play on the album and I asked famed producer and multi-instrumentalist Ricky Fataar to play on a few tracks. We wanted to produce a quality album and wanted every song to be strong.

Brian is my music buddy, drinking buddy and is like a brother to me; he's also a very clever people person who knows how to work a room. Having run his own label, his knowledge of the music business is very strong, which is something I've struggled with over the years. He's also very pragmatic and an excellent songwriter who loves a good hook and a quirky turn of phrase.

'The Salads' became somewhat well-known at the local liquor store by cleaning them out of the Côtes du Rhône, which was regarded by the good ol' boys in the south as 'cat's piss'. I was interested in new technology and Brian was already using it in his

upstairs studio, which we named 'the Salad Bowl'. Using Apple apps, we were able to produce an album that was fun to write and perform, and we were well pleased with our efforts. We built the album from the ground up and it was of the best projects I've been involved in. I know it may sound pompous but the concept and creativity of such a project is the essence of why I do it ... the rest can become drudgery. Not so the Salads!

Lo and behold, our EMI benefactor Brian Harris decided to

Brian and Jo are very close and we have all been great mates over the years.

go to WEA, thereby robbing us of the important mentor we needed to get the record into the market. We released *When It All Comes Down* on Blue Martin Records in 1994 and crossed our fingers. Hampered by the fact that we did not use our real names, the album failed to click with the public but has become a 'collector's item' over the years. I am still very proud of it.

Blazing Salads toured while LRB were on sabbatical, to small but enthusiastic crowds. I played my hit songs, along with those of Axiom, accompanied by Cadd on piano and a backing band of Rex Goh (guitar), Kirk Lorange (guitar) and veteran Spectrum and Ayers Rock drummer Mark Kennedy. A decade later we recorded a compilation of our best work under the title *The Story Of Sharky & The Caddman*. We never learn!

In 1995 LRB marked our twentieth anniversary (baby!), which seemed to be good reason to go on the road again. Wayne had indicated he was coping better and he felt he could perform again. A thirty-four-track double CD had been compiled by John Boylan and Derek Pellicci for Capitol/EMI and we had a new agent, Steve Green, out of Boca Raton, Florida, who put together a gruelling tour beginning in May and ending in September, some eighty-eight shows in all.

We took five crew with us, including Chris Newman and Noel Bennett from Australia, and three Americans. We rehearsed in LA for three days then flew to Pennsylvania for the first gig and

With co-owners of Kele Kele, our friends Lionel and Judy Hunt after a day's successful fishing.

then down to Atlanta where we picked up our beloved stage coach, driven up from Florida by Joe Mullins, and headed on down the road, as they say in the business!

The next four and a half months were a bit of a blur, crisscrossing the country in the heat of the summer playing a variety of venues including a lot of state fairs, beloved by Midwest folk. We would often arrive in our bus and make it our base for the day, enjoying the 'cornball' but friendly atmosphere of the fair, do the show and leave on the bus overnighting to the next state fair, partying all the way.

I was signing autographs after one state fair and the naiveté of some fans never failed to surprise me. 'Glenn, we have all your records, don't we Margaret? Could you sign the album please ... darling here and I love your song, "Cool Chance"!' I resisted the temptation to ask them if they had heard 'Home On A Tuesday'! I can be a sarcastic bugger.

When Derek and Stephen came to talk to me the following year about another tour of the US, they wanted a six-month commitment from me but I said I would do three months at most. Jo's mother was suffering from the advanced stages of dementia, and my dad had a stroke after a routine knee operation and had also been hospitalised, and we didn't want to be away from our families for that long.

Derek and Steve, my fellow directors of LRB, insisted I agree to six months or they would go on without me and with a new singer. I couldn't believe this was happening to me again and the meeting ended abruptly. I was replaced by Steve Wade, who gladly took over wearing the beret I had adopted, and off they went to the US, leaving me in a pretty angry state. My relationship with Derek has never repaired.

The sad thing is, when LRB first formed Derek and I hit it off straight away and developed a great relationship over the years. On tour, we often took on the role of dealing with most of the promotion and press calls, along with Beeb, because Derek had the gift of the gab, as did I, and we had a lot of fun together.

At that time Jo's mother Vera needed constant attention from her family and Jo was with her many days and nights. Vera was a wonderful woman who raised six children and Jo, the youngest of the family, wanted to be closer to her in Melbourne to care for her in her final years.

We looked at an apartment being built above the old Botanical Hotel in Domain Road, South Yarra and bought on the second floor, with a roof terrace that looked across to Melbourne's lovely Botanical Gardens. We moved in with our Blue Heeler Doc, having lost our cocker spaniel to pancreatic cancer while I was away on tour.

The Anchorage was rented to Mark Booth and family, who was brought to Australia to set up the Foxtel company. Consequently, we were one of the first households to be connected to this new entertainment service. 'The Bot', as the Melbourne apartment became known, was ideally situated for us, the tram stopping across the road. The city gardens became our gardens and we walked Doc almost every day through its exotic landscapes. Below us was our favourite feeding and watering hole, run by old Greek friends Christos and Harry. We had lucked out again!

I was getting more and more work in and around Melbourne at that time, plus some great corporate gigs abroad, and I hooked up with some local musos who became firm friends.

Soon after our relocation back to Melbourne (in 1996), I was walking in the gardens when I ran into Glen Elston who was producing *A Midsummer Night's Dream* in an open-air theatre. He also had recently taken over the Comedy Club in Carlton, and we got talking about doing some theatre again. I came up with a show based on duets in pop and I asked Wendy Stapleton to join me in a show we called *Two Up*. Wendy was great fun to work with. The show was similar to *One For The Money* and we had great fun frocking up as Sonny and Cher and John and Yoko! I played giggling Yoko to Wendy's John behind a life-size photo of the *Two Virgins* nude album cover! The show worked well for a month or so, despite the amount of alcohol being consumed at that time. The fact that we actually lived over our friend's restaurant was both a blessing and a curse but at least our apartment was a very short crawl up the stairs.

Vera Swan passed away in early 1997. My mother-in-law was much loved by her family, and by me, and was a woman who was full of grace and tolerance towards others.

Meanwhile, my father Harry was admitted into a nursing home for a similar reason back in Adelaide. Harry was in his early eighties by then and had suffered a minor stroke while

One of the last photos of the Shorrock family together back in Adelaide before my father's illness in the late 1990s. They made a great life for themselves there.

under anaesthetic during a knee operation. Dad's decline was sad to behold, both mentally and physically, having been such a bright and fit man all his life but there were moments of lucidity. On one of my visits to him, we sat in the sunshine and discussed the state of his health. One symptom of the medication he was on was enlarged testicles and the conversation went something like this:

Me: How are you feeling Dad?

Harry: Okay. (silence)

Me: How's your stomach ache?

Harry: Okay. (long silence)

Me: How are your balls, Dad?

Harry: Okay. How are yours?

******

Towards the end of the decade, SEL (Sports Entertainment Limited) and the Gordon Frost Organisation were putting together *Grease: The Arena Spectacular* and offered me the role of Johnny Casino alongside other cameos: Anthony Warlow as Teen Angel and Doug Parkinson as Vince Fontaine, with Craig McLachlan, Jane Scali and Dannii Minogue in the lead roles of Danny, Sandy and Rizzo. It was the biggest musical ever presented in Australia in the largest arenas in the country.

I signed a deal negotiated by my old manager Glenn Wheatley for sixteen shows with an increasing fee corresponding to when shows were added. The show was such a success we ending up doing seventy-two shows in front of nearly 750,000 people, which pleased all of us including my bank manager. The cast was over fifty strong – all young and wonderfully talented people. The show was presented in the round with the band 'flown' above the main stage in a sort of flying saucer (with a small bucket for emergencies!).

Doug and I shared a dressing room for the duration; we

played a lot of cards and told a lot of lies as we only had one song each in the second half of the show. It was a most impressive production and I thank Mr Wheatley for negotiating such a sweetheart deal for me. For one song!

******

The second side of the Beatles' classic 1969 album *Abbey Road*, has long been a favourite of mine. For me, it's a true piece of symphonic rock and deserves to be placed alongside iconic works of Gershwin and Berlin, Bach or Beethoven. I knew George Martin had performed some of the scores he'd written for the classic Beatles tunes with orchestras in Europe so I contacted him with the idea of performing the Abbey Road 'suite' and a collection of other great songs such as 'Penny Lane', 'Strawberry Fields' and 'I Am The Walrus', alongside an all-star Australian band.

The first question George asked was whether we would play the Sydney Opera House? I told him of course, and he said, 'Then I shall come!' Fantastic! With the help of the Hocking and Woods Company, I produced the show *All You Need Is Beatles* over six concerts in early 1998, with the Brisbane Youth Orchestra, and the Sydney and Melbourne Symphony Orchestras. I secured the Farnham band (minus John) to provide the backing and 'the frontline' consisted of myself, Tommy Emmanuel, James Reyne and Human Nature as featured vocalists. Of course, we were led by George (by then Sir George) Martin conducting his magical scores of those wonderful Beatles classics. Having a vodka martini with him before each show was a special 'settling of nerves' ritual.

It was an amazing time and we were all in awe of the great man in action. To this day, it is the best thing I have ever done in my career, to have worked alongside George. Some years later, I had the honour of hosting the launch of his book *Playback*,

On stage with the great man, Sir George Martin, in 1998 for the *All You Need is Beatles* show. Also pictured is James Reyne (middle) and one of the guys from Human Nature, who also were

216

in the production. Sir George would come in on the morning of a show and greet them with a cheery, 'Good Morning Humans' … he was a lovely man.

a lavish publication that described his recording years, and my copy bears his signature. A photo of him looks down at me from the wall in my study as I write this. The man who changed pop music forever is sadly missed today.

Thank you, George, for all you did for us in our careers and particularly, 'in my life'.

CHAPTER 17

Boats, Planes and Reasonably Fast Cars

'It's kind of a special feeling when you're out on the sea alone ...' It's also good to have some great players around you too. In 1999, I had a job aboard the *Norwegian Star*. The trip was brokered by Graeme Gillies who owns Grayboy, a company that represents a lot of musical theatre artists and produces entertainment shows for sea cruises. The *Norwegian Star* is by now being broken down for scrap on a beach somewhere in India. She was a rather elegant seventies ship and an early entrant into the cruising scene here in Australia. Graeme was a young performer on board before becoming a cruise director. Having enjoyed a long and influential history with sea travel I was eager to get my 'feet wet' again.

My first voyage introduced me to the Skelton Brothers, Mick and David, who were in the ship's band. They were a group of versatile young performers led by Cruise Director Gerry Gallagher, who was steeped in vaudeville schtick from years of working on ships and treading the boards back in England. I warmed to him immediately, as did Jo, and we still enjoy his company from time to time with the Gillies family. Graeme married Melinda, one of the ship's talented performers, and they have more emerging talent in their children Coco, Rupert and Evie.

For eighteen years now, I've enjoyed working for P&O Cruises

At the Adelaide Grand Prix, during my 'early racing career'. I took part in the celebrity race and absolutely loved the experience, another childhood ambition of becoming a racing driver realised.

and Carnival, thanks to Grayboy, and more recently Celebrity Cruises and Mick Manov and Marius Els, who put together theme cruises such as 'Rock The Boat', which I've done a few times. It helps, of course, that Marius is also my agent. The cruise business is growing into the most popular way of holidaying and no wonder, as the modern ships are virtually floating resorts and offer a wide range of choices.

We live on the harbour in Sydney and watch with interest the comings and goings of liners of all shapes and sizes. Nowadays, Sydney is a vital stop for over 300 ships per year and new berthing facilities are needed as this number increases. Back in the fifties and sixties when I was 'commuting' to the UK and back, most vessels doubled as cargo ships as well as passenger liners. The Twilights and later Axiom played for our passage in cramped, six-berth cabins and the equipment on board was primitive compared to today, where fully functioning theatres are on most boats. I'm sure my cruising days are not over for me, as a performer and a 'guest', as passengers are now known.

Of course, air travel has become part of my life as well as a means to get to where I need to go but I've yet to perform on a flight, although the Airbus A380 could accommodate a small lounge band like Los Trios (note to Qantas). Flying is still a mystical way to get around; I mean how does one of those huge things even get off the ground? So far, I've escaped having an incident in the air and have enjoyed flying first class and in the back, depending on distance and who's paying.

In the LRB days on one journey from LA to Hawaii, the airline was featuring 'pub flights' with a small bar on board. I and my manservant/lighting director Peter Rooney succumbed to drinks that must have been spiked with LSD by a couple of surfies on their way to Waimea Bay. Needless to say, we became the entertainment and irritation on board and it continued after landing, in what became known as our 'Hawaii Five-O' incident. We spent the next twelve hours looking for Jack Lord in and around our hotel in Honolulu, to no avail ... even checking laundry shutes.

Trains can also be a fine way of getting around, mostly in a non-professional capacity, but I fondly remember the London tube taking me to and from work, when I had some, especially the shows at the Palladium with Cliff Richard in the 1970s. I did, however, do my time as a commuter on the District Line, trying not to make eye contact with the skinhead sitting opposite on my way home to Tulse Hill.

Cars have always greatly interested me. I had a small collection

of Dinky models as a young boy and I remember Aunty Madeline had an Austin Atlantic at the time, an English model trying hard to look like an American car. As a teenager I was in a hurry to learn to drive, mainly because it was a good way to pick up girls (intended pun). My father taught me to drive in his Ford Consul, the cheaper cousin of the Zephyr and Zodiac. Dad instilled in me that a good driver is one who makes his passengers enjoy the journey too, so smoothness matters. I got my licence as soon as my sixteenth birthday had passed. In those days in South Australia, one got a licence just by passing a written test no driving skills tested!

Lynda and our mother Joyce at back with dear Carol Birnie in the front seat of my Alpine.

I bought my first car with a little help from Mum and Dad – a 1954 VW Beetle (the one with the small rear window). It quickly became my 'passion wagon' and could be seen rocking gently when stationary at various locations around Adelaide; mainly drive-in movie theatres, actually.

I was once driving back to Mum and Dad's having dropped

off my current girlfriend after a sweaty session at the Elizabeth Shandon, a then mecca for teenagers, and swerved suddenly to avoid a head-on with a car being driven without headlights on. The result was a roll over, leaving me flung into the back seat but uninjured. The Beetle was on its side in the middle of the road close to home when who should arrive but Dad, coming home from night shift. He quickly appraised the situation and helped me push the car back on its wheels, then saw that it started and said, 'I'll see you at home lad,' and left me to it. I've never had an accident since other than a few bumps and scratches.

All my mates were into mostly English sports cars. I soon swapped the dented Beetle for a 1948 white MG TC with 18-inch wire wheels and started wearing driving gloves and flat caps. I was still only seventeen or so, and the duco on the TC was a little worse for wear. I knew a red car was a fast car so I bought a can of auto paint and a brush and hand-painted it myself. My older, purist car-buff mates were horrified but I thought it did go faster, if you call 75 miles per hour fast!

I flung it around the Adelaide Hills for a year or so then saw

My sister Lynda and her friend Bev sitting in my Triumph TR3.

an ad for a Triumph TR3 and traded the 'G' in for a much cooler set of wheels which fitted better with the vehicles of my fellow members of the Elizabeth Sports Car Club. We called ourselves that to gain some respectability while chasing each other through the Mount Lofty Ranges and elsewhere in the state. You could drive onto Moana Beach in those days and pretend it was Daytona Florida!

My Nissan Skyline GT I drove to Melbourne in after relocating there with the Twilights in 1966.

As my level of sophistication grew, I progressed to a Sunbeam Alpine and just before I left Adelaide I bought my first new car, a Nissan Skyline GT. While in England with the Twilights the car was repossessed, having been looked after by a friend. All I could manage after that was a Morris Minor and finally the indignity of a Lambretta scooter.

By 1977 I could afford me an Alfa Romeo GTV then moved through two BMW 7 series. I now drive an Audi Cabriolet and Mercedes 250 Sport. Limos, of course, became the mode of travel for a few years in the US and I've had a few adventures

in those when we were riding high in the charts, as they say.

Today, I rarely use public transport and my driving time is dwindling mainly because the traffic in Sydney is *not*, parking is a pain and prices are a rip-off. Oh, for some Wilson's shares!

I make no secret when I say I'm a bit of a petrol head. My boyhood heroes were Stirling Moss and Fangio and I've followed Formula One ever since. So, when I was invited to compete in the celebrity race at the Adelaide Grand Prix in the late 1980s I embraced it with relish and trained at a rough track near Salisbury to gain a temporary CAMS licence. We all raced in little Nissan Exa Coupes and I managed to finish in the top ten. The next year I got on the podium in third place driving a BMW and setting the fastest lap of the race. One of my rivals was pole sitter Mark Knopfler from Dire Straits who had some racing experience in the UK and is a lovely chap. He was shocked when passed at the start by someone who 'jumped the gun' under the advice from ex-World Champ Alan Jones. In an overreaction, Mark tried to regain the lead but put his car into the wall on the first corner and fractured his collarbone, much to the horror of the promoter of his upcoming tour!

Jo and me at the Grand Prix Ball in 1991 with Glenn and Gaynor Wheatley (on left) and champion golfer Wayne Grady (centre). Glenn was managing Wayne at the time I think, and we all became great mates.

In another race, at the Indy Car meet on the Gold Coast, I had a ding-dong battle with old friend Richard Wilkins. He and I swapped the lead three times but we crossed the line together with Dicky scraping in by half a car length!

I was offered a drive in a minor local league driving for Mitsubishi but couldn't commit because weekends were when I was working mostly. I did, however, get to sit in Schumacher's old Ferrari for a photo publicising Birtles Shorrock Goble's performance at the 2003 Melbourne Grand Prix Ball.

So I get my rocks off as a virtual racing driver these days via video games. I have won the Formula One World Championships many times over, albeit virtually, and have been threatened with divorce many times because of it. I remain fascinated with the creativity of the video games that are available. I had already tried the *Prince Of Persia* game but when I was introduced to *Myst* while doing the *Blazing Salads* album I was hooked and played it long into the night after recording sessions. I am of the opinion that in these times, the creative high ground is largely taken up by computer game designers who rival movie producers in expertise, although both genres are now coming together and repeating a well-trodden formula aimed at fifteen-year-old boys.

CHAPTER 18

The New Millennium

As the old century drew to a close, Jo and I sadly said goodbye to the Botanical, and also to our trusty blue healer dog Doc, and moved back to the Anchorage in Sydney to await the new millennium. It had been widely anticipated that a worldwide computer virus would strike us all, plunging the world back into the dark ages. Being an amateur prophet of doom, I took an eager interest in proceedings and bought a box of pigeons just in case, to help keep contact with the anticipated decimated world.

The new year came, thankfully, without the conflagration predicted. I said goodbye to the old century with thanks and a nice Grenache on our roof terrace. Almost two decades later, my electronic devices are still working, if somewhat frustratingly sporadically, and the pigeons have all been lost or eaten.

In 1998, our friend Chez wanted to check out an apartment that she thought looked beautiful and so Jo and I went with her. What we saw made a big impression on us both – a wonderful harbourside apartment in a heritage building in Double Bay. A financial adviser at the time convinced us to bite the bullet and put a deposit down and put the Anchorage on the market.

Selling the Anchorage took some time as we sold it as two titles but we managed to get a satisfactory price and in January 2000 we moved ourselves into our Eastern Suburbs residence. Architectural elegance and modern living side by side, and on a water frontage, were so important to us after twenty years at

Have song, will travel … more than thirty years on stage and still going strong into the new millennium. (Courtesy Bob King)

beautiful Birchgrove. I was moved to recognise my journey from post-War England to a home in one of the most prestigious addresses in Australia.

As the new millennium ticked over the big world was going through some massive changes and this was reflected in changes to my little world. In April 2001, Harry Shorrock passed away quietly. The illness reduced him physically and the man I kissed goodbye in his coffin no longer looked like my dad; to me he had taken on the look of an American Indian chief. We had a beautiful ceremony for him and his remains lie under a rose bush in Mum's garden.

I am proud of my mum and dad; he was a typical Yorkshireman – funny, stoic and very pragmatic to the point of being unemotional (some would say, like his son). He kept his opinion of my career close to his chest, however, only twice seeing me in a live performance. The last time was when I persuaded him to attend a Little River Band concert with the Adelaide Symphony Orchestra at the Festival Theatre because there would be violins. The next morning, I greeted him at the family home for breakfast:

Me: Morning Dad.

Harry: Morning.

Me: So, what did you think?

Harry: About what?

Me: The concert, Dad.

Harry: Oh aye. It were grand seeing you up there but it were too loud. You don't have to have it that loud do you? There was one thing that puzzled me though. What were those big packing cases on either side of the stage? Were they to pack the drums in?'

He was talking about the PA speakers.

Did I mention that Harry also had a fine baritone voice and that he introduced me to the finest operatic arias of the century, from Caruso to Pavarotti? His favourite, and, mine is 'Torna a Surriento'.

I regret that we had little time together, man to man, after I left the family home, somewhat selfishly, at the age of nineteen, but he was a great dad. I see him every morning in the mirror.

About that time, Brian Cadd had ended his marriage to Lynda and was now with another Linda on the Gold Coast in Mudgeeraba and had installed a studio there, aptly named Gingerman Studio. I recorded an album with him there called *Spin Me Round* with local musicians, and the rest of the album was reinforced with some LRB hits and two songs from *Villain Of The Peace*. One of the Nashvillian submissions was an early Keith Urban song, 'At The Mercy Of The Sea', a little gem in my opinion. Our friend Vanetta Fields, a veteran of the '20 feet from stardom' syndrome, sang a duet with me on 'Dixie Wire'. It was a great experience all round but the album received little to no airplay.

Houghton Hall house guests in Norfolk, East Anglia; (from left) Jasper Conran, Francesco Boglione, me, Eski Thomas, Sabrina Guinness and Gael Boglione. (Jo took this photo)

Then, in August 2001, we were shocked to hear that ex-Skyhooks singer Graeme 'Shirley' Strachan had been killed in a freak helicopter accident when he was flying in southern Queensland. I liked him a lot and we were all saddened to lose a vibrant personality with such honesty when it came to judging himself and others. His memorial concert was held at the St Kilda Palais, the place was packed and we were treated to an emotional show with a reformed Skyhooks, with guest singers including their close friend and mentor Ross Wilson.

After the show John Farnham, Glenn and Gaynor Wheatley, and Jo and I carried on into the night. After a long dinner, we went back the Wheatleys and just after midnight Jill Farnham rang John, crying down the phone. 'Just turn on the television!' she said without explanation.

What we saw appeared to be a disaster movie playing out on live TV. It took a short while to realise we were watching live coverage of the World Trade Center attacks in New York. John immediately excused himself and rushed home to be with his family. We could not believe what we were seeing and were glued to the screen as the disaster worsened. I watched the TV coverage until the sun came up, feeling that the world would never be the same again ... and it hasn't been. The 'War on Terror' began that day and we all applauded. I don't hear too much cheering now.

In 2002, I was approached by Amanda Pelman, on behalf of legendary promoter Michael Chugg, to join the 'cast of thousands' in a stadium tour of Australia. Based on the 2001 documentary series *Long Way To The Top*, the tour showcased the stars from the different eras of Australian rock 'n' roll, from Col Joye in the 1950s to Billy Thorpe and the Aztecs in the 1960s and '70s. They wanted to reform the Twilights and Axiom so it sounded like a lot of fun. Little did I know just how much fun it was going to be. Thorpie later said it was a month-long party interrupted every night by a performance.

Billy Thorpe was also the creative producer, alongside

Amanda. One of the fond memories of that tour was that we forgot about past rivalries and really enjoyed each other's company. I found that I could make him laugh and that became our common ground.

The house band led by Jamie Rigg backed most artists, including the 'Long Way' Twilights, which consisted of myself, Paddy McCartney, John Bywaters and Peter Brideoake. Terry Britten decided not to join us (he lives in England) and Laurie Prior had died a couple of years before.

Axiom was just Brian and myself but we were joined by seventeen other legends, including Billy Thorpe, Stevie Wright, Normie Rowe, John Paul Young, Russell Morris, Ross Wilson, Marcia Hines, Doug Parkinson and the Masters Apprentices. Premier chanteuse Renée Geyer was asked to guest star on a few shows, replacing Marcia, who was unavailable. Her voice always wowed us and the audience but sadly, she had a physical confrontation with Amanda Pelman backstage and was sent packing. I did not witness the incident but someone said it looked like two seagulls fighting over a chip!

Needless to say, the public loved it, and the show ended each night with a somewhat chaotic tribute to AC/DC, with the title song sung by a plethora of egos, Billy being the main flag bearer. We all then behaved badly into the night at various lobby bars, startling both guests and staff. I was found one night asleep outside the lifts on the 11th floor of the Melbourne Hilton, having been unable to remember which room I was in. Enough said.

A few years later, *Long Way To The Top* went out into the provinces for a tour under the big top. On the road the show was a kind of a 'Magical Mystery Tour'. I usually travelled on the bus with the other 'veterans' … mind you the whole line up were the same so the level of larrikinism was high. Col Joye became our emotional father. He would travel with a ukulele and encouraged us to sing Vera Lynn songs, which was a fun for about thirty minutes. Doug Parkinson reminded everyone of the definition or 'perfect pitch' – to be able to throw a ukulele down the toilet without hitting the sides ... and Col didn't take the hint.

'We'll meet again, don't know where, don't know when ...'

In 2004, I was touring with Birtles Shorrock Goble and recorded a live performance for a DVD over two nights in the wonderful old rococo building, The Forum in Melbourne. As I bowed for the last time I saw to my left Mike Munro, the host of *This Is Your Life* hovering in the wings. The audience were invited to stay and watch the taping of the program but I just wanted to get to my dressing room and pop a nice Shiraz! We got out of there at 2 am.

It was a tough, exhausting night but I was flattered by the attention from my peers and loved ones and rolled with the punches. One of my guests was flown in from Fiji, our much loved Finau, our housekeeper from Kele Kele on Wakaya. Jo had negotiated with Channel Nine and spoken with the record company to facilitate the promotion of BSG's forthcoming *Full Circle* DVD. Unfortunately, this didn't happen and the record company bought only one TV spot – for a cool $80,000!

The night became an emotional roller coaster for everyone involved, especially me. We eventually found ourselves back in our suite at Crown Towers with Billy Thorpe and Doug Parkinson, two well-known carousers, although Doug was then sober, and still is. Billy, however, was not, and when he ordered champagne on my room tab and was cautioned, he began a well-worn tirade, this time aimed at Jo, and we had to ask him to leave. What a night! That was Billy at his most obnoxious; the worst version of himself.

The *Long Way To The Top* tour reconvened and I found Thorpie much more amenable and we actually had a good time together. Although he never did apologise for what was said to Jo, we put it all behind us. Billy passed away soon after, in early 2007, at the young age of sixty, and I remember him kindly. He was a huge figure in Australian music; an original.

Former Easybeat Stevie Wright was another legend to make

In a Spanish hotel in Saville (not a barber to be found!). What's in the crystal ball for me?

that tour a farewell of sorts. It was with a sad heart that we all went to his funeral a few years ago. Stevie had struggled with drug addiction for over forty years and the ceremony in St Andrews Cathedral was the most moving funeral that I've been to and I've been to far too many in recent years. I estimate there were about 2000 mourners there to farewell him. Safe travels mate.

In 2005, Brisbane entrepreneur Robert Clark, who was once a percussionist with the Queensland Symphony, wanted to tour a show in the eastern states with a small orchestra. I agreed but it felt risky to me. I asked old friends Wendy Matthews and Doug Parkinson to join me in what would be called 'The Reminiscing Tour'. The show was put together on a shoestring budget, charts were done by John Woodend, who played tenor sax in the show, and the 'orchestra' consisted of four strings, four brass, one keyboard, one percussion and the frontline band of two guitars, bass, drums and piano!

With Wendy, Doug and me on the frontlines, with Robert Clark conducting, this totalled seventeen people on stage. I wanted to present a great musical show but we felt the strain financially. Robert was somewhat naive and treated the show as his own, conducting with over enthusiasm much to the irritation of the hardened veterans amongst us. There were moments of farce, one of which involved Robert counting the musicians into a softer number with 'One, two, three, shhh, four!' but there were some goosebumps vocal moments from the three principals and we did have our usual fun on the road. The inevitable happened and we finished prematurely but I do like to take on a challenge sometimes.

The following year, I had the chance to perform in a Beatles tribute show around Australia and New Zealand. 'Let It Be' was a labour of love for me and I took great satisfaction that the concerts pleased audiences on both sides of the Tasman. Sharon O'Neill, Mark Williams and the always wonderful Doug Parkinson joined in the fun.

New Zealand has long been a favourite destination of ours and is high on our list of places to one day retire to, along with Fiji. I first went to New Zealand with the Twilights in 1966 when 'Needle In A Haystack' was number one, way back when, and I've enjoyed touring there ever since. I've seen that lovely country from top to bottom, from the Bay of Islands to Invercargill. The South Island is my choice, although it can be bloody cold. Jo and I have skied Queenstown often and spent time with friends in Nelson, a gorgeous secret hideaway. It's a great country to drive around too, and the food and people are first class.

The sheet music for 'Cool Change', with Barry Sullivan (front left) and Mal Logan (back, centre) joining LRB on tour.

Musically, the Kiwis have punched above their weight for decades and have produced such great artists as Max Merritt and the Meteors in the sixties, right up to Lorde today. One of my favourite singer-songwriters from the 'Shaky Isles' is Dave Dobbyn, closely followed by the various incarnations of the Finn brothers, Neil and Tim. I have enjoyed my own success there too and the Kiwis love 'Cool Change', it's a bit of an anthem over there.

My other fond memory of the 'Let It Be' tour was performing one of my favourite Beatles songs, 'Penny Lane', the song the lads were recording while the Twilights were next door at Abbey Road more than fifty years ago. Paul Thorne played the iconic piccolo trumpet solo in 'Penny Lane' on that tour. Paul is a wine aficionado, which is another term for loving a good time! Every evening we held our breath on stage as the climactic note approached. Bets were placed either way but most nights he nailed it. That was another example of on-stage fellowship that I'm so fond of.

At the end of 2007, I was asked to join the cast of *Shout! The Legend Of The Wild One*, a new production based on the life of Johnny O'Keefe and directed by Stuart Maunder from Opera Australia. Tim Campbell starred as Johnny O'Keefe, along with Mark Holden as Lee Gordon, John Paul Young in various cameo roles, Colleen Hewett as JO'K's mum and yours truly as his father! We rehearsed for six weeks in Melbourne and opened on 4 January, 2008, at the Arts Centre. After that we played the Lyric Theatre in the Star Casino complex in Sydney.

I met JO'K for about ten minutes in the late 1970s. I didn't see him as a singer as much as a live performer and rabble-rouser on stage. The irony is, I tried out for the JO'K miniseries in the early 1980s but was deemed to be 'too old' and the role went to Terry Serio. It just goes to show that if you stay around long enough, if you don't get the main role you can later play their father!

John Paul Young and I had 'digs' in the same hotel in St Kilda Road and were able to walk to work conveniently and hang out after. I enjoyed the role and the wig supplied but I was dressed accordingly as a fifties father in grey pants and a cardigan, saying things like 'good gracious' and 'strewth!', whereas Tim played a taller Johnny in various satin, leopard skin outfits. Colleen relished being my stage wife and gave me heaps when I missed a cue once and entered from the wrong side in a scene. JPY was brilliant in about five or six cameo roles and showed me another side to his talent; to my mind he stole the show. Once again, I had the pleasure of joining a great production team and cast, all of whom had a great time. Fellowship again?

******

Somebody who was definitely not having a great time then was Glenn Wheatley. Glenn had been badly misled and advised and had become a scapegoat in a scandal that enveloped many others, including Paul Hogan, who decided to fight the accusations from his Los Angeles home. Several prominent Australians were implicated in off-shore tax-evasion schemes and the Australian Tax Office's Project Wickenby needed a high-profile scalp. Enter Glenn Wheatley.

Found guilty, Glenn was sentenced to thirty months in jail, with a minimum fifteen months to be served. His name and

reputation were in tatters and so started a very dark time for the Wheatley family as he began his incarceration in Beechworth Correctional Centre in northern Victoria. Glenn's wife Gaynor and his family began weekly visits to him along with various supporters, often including Jo and myself. He did what he could to get through his time but it was tough. He worked in the prison garden for some of the time and grew produce for the kitchen.

Gaynor's life was one of total commitment in support of Glenn and we were all behind her. She was his 'rock'. After his release in May 2008, he was able to complete his sentence in home detention but his house was always under surveillance by media eager to drive the nails in further. Glenn has slowly rebuilt his career with the help of his close friend John Farnham and he has embarked on various business ventures. Over the last few years, he was still hounded by the ATO until recently when the tax office itself came under scrutiny for spending millions of dollars in pursuit of unpaid taxes and the pressure was suddenly lifted from Glenn's shoulders.

My relationship with Glenn has survived many ups and downs because of the girls in our lives; Jo and Gaynor are thick as thieves and we are very close to the Wheatleys' children. He's made some mistakes courting the high end of town and listened to the wrong people but it was a terrible time when he was in jail and we all felt for the family. The whole ten-year ordeal is now over and although he has been damaged to a certain extent, Glenn's positive energy and prodigious work ethic is admirable.

Two of my favourite people, Gael Boglione and Gaynor Wheatley. Gael is Jo's oldest friend and Gaynor Jo's closest friend in Australia.

CHAPTER 19

Weddings, Parties, Anything

I have been very happy during my career being a creative 'dragonfly', going from flower to flower so to speak: hosting the Mike Walsh *Midday Show,* acting in *The Paul Hogan Show,* trying out for the lead in a biopic on Australia's original 'Wild One', Johnny O'Keefe.

I suppose I always wanted to be an all-round entertainer, as the great Peter Sellers (aka 'Twit Conway') once opined in the following comedy skit:

> Reporter: Well, Twit, do you want to stay a rock 'n' roll singer all your life? I mean, what is your ultimate ambition?
>
> Twit: (pause) Er, we are just good friends.
>
> Major: (interrupting) That is the answer to another question! Remember? The answer to this one is: I want to become an all-round ...
>
> Twit: Oh yeah! Er, I wantter become an all-round.
>
> Major: (whispering) Entertainer!
>
> Twit: Er, entertainer, yeah. Um, my dream is one day to play Old Vic in Shakespeare.
>
> Reporter: Oh, how sweet! You are fond of Shakespeare?
>
> Twit: Er, we are just good friends.

GS, 2007.

(Courtesy Tony Mott)

In the mid-1980s, and free of LRB, I was contacted by comedian Paul Hogan with the offer of appearing in his next TV series. I had done some work with Paul in 1979 and had a lot of laughs with Hoges, John 'Strop' Cornell and a bevy of semi-dressed women. It was a shame he didn't give me a call when he was casting the film *Crocodile Dundee*, that would have been fun.

Not that this would have been the first film I had tried out for. In the early 1970s when I was living in London, I tried out for a part in Bruce Beresford's *The Adventures Of Barry McKenzie*. I missed out on the part of Bazza's mate Curly but would have loved to have worked with Barry Crocker and Barry Humphries, a hero of mine, on that film. I recently completed a part in a small 'indie' film written and directed by Sasha Hadden called *Liebe* that we hope to see released soon, so watch this space.

Another string to my bow was to serve as a writer/director on the Board of Australian Performing Rights Association

On stage with famous producer Quincy Jones at the APRA Awards in the 1990s. Jones was affable enough but taciturn ... he had little to say to anyone (including me as host!).

(APRA) for eighteen years. I hosted a few APRA Awards as well, and one I remember had Quincy Jones alongside me. I was with APRA when we went to Washington DC to attend a convention hosted by CISAC (the International Confederation of Societies of Authors and Composers) to mark a significant anniversary of copyright ownership, the mechanics of which still confuse me to this day. Jo and I enjoyed the experience, which included visiting the Smithsonian Institute and attending a concert on the lawns of the White House occupied, at that time by a little-known saxophonist named Bill Clinton. A mini cyclone hit Washington that night and turned the lawns into a quagmire into which the guests sank but the dinner and show featured some iconic American talent including Lyall Lovett and Booker T and the MGs. I got into the White House just briefly to relieve myself and we all had ruined shoes.

Over the years, my services have been used to entertain at private functions, charity balls and the like. They have been a significant part of my career and have taken me to some interesting venues, from beaches to aircraft carriers. I've always been in demand performing my body of work to my contemporaries, people who have grown up with my music and have often become high achievers in the corporate world and hired me for their functions here and abroad. Most have been enjoyable and lucrative, some have been bizarre.

One that comes to mind was a new year's eve party staged in the Sheraton Hotel in Phuket Thailand. I was booked by the

Working with comedian Paul Hogan on *The Paul Hogan Show* in the 1980s ... a splendid time is guaranteed for all!

managing director (an Australian) who had been a fan. However, when the time came he had been moved on and replaced by an Austrian MD who had no idea who I was but had been given the heads up by his predecessor. Jo and I travelled business class and we were all accommodated in two beautiful five-star, three-bedroom villas in the hotel grounds for four nights and took advantage of all the resort facilities. We had the use of buggies and bikes around the compound and use of all restaurants. We started to notice a lot of burly looking men escorting attractive young girls who spoke in thick European accents and were informed that a large percentage of the guests were Russian 'businessmen' and they had brought their 'secretaries' along.

We were contracted to play two sets up to the midnight moment and beyond. The Russians gradually settled into their tables drinking champagne and vodka and it was more than evident they had no interest in our music whatsoever. So, I turned to the band and yelled '"Back in the USSR" boys!' and we launched into the Beatles classic. It did the trick and the Russians began to dance, lurching around the previously rather empty dance floor. As soon as we finished they wanted more so we played the song again to rapturous applause.

'We got 'em,' I mouthed to the band. Suddenly, the clock ticked over to midnight, the fireworks went off and so did our newly acquired audience. The marquee on the beach emptied in seconds and we were left to sing 'Auld Lang Syne' to the Thai waiters, who seemed to enjoy it at least.

We soon joined in with the vodka fest into the new year; even a few abandoned 'babushkas' took a keen interest in certain members of the band and, I dare say, myself, although those big Bolshevik boyfriends looked a bit threatening. The next day, all was forgiven and we were the toast of the Kremlin. We later frolicked in the ocean with young Thai elephants brought to the sea to bathe, which was a nice experience.

Billionaire Richard Pratt also liked to turn it on for his

staff around Australia and New Zealand at Christmas time and became a generous client and friend. I did seven shows one year for him along with Marcia Hines. Dick thought of himself as a singer as well and opened the show with a version of Peter Allen's 'I Still Call Australia Home'. A charming man, as a singer he was a brilliant businessman (which he was!).

Clive Palmer, literally one of Australia's largest tycoons at the time, was also a long-time fan of mine. We were booked to play at his fifteen-year-old daughter's birthday party at the Palazzo Versace hotel on the Gold Coast, probably the most sumptuous hotel in the country – well suited for a teenager's birthday. I later learnt that her present from Dad was the penthouse in the hotel!

Clive had all her classmates and their parents stay there as his guests. I was puzzled by the appearance in front of my young audience, as they were by me, but it went down well with the parents! In our dressing room, we found M&Ms and Coca Cola, and for our opening act, a young band of boys, obviously friends of the birthday girl, who went down better than we did! We met the host that night, and later when we were alone he outlined grandiose plans that included for me to produce and host a concert at the Albert Hall, with an Australian flavour. Could I get Eric Clapton and Elton John as guests, he asked? I told him I thought it was out of my league but he persisted for a while until something else took his attention.

I worked again for Clive Palmer at the Hyatt in Coolum at a Christmas Party for his staff alongside Leo Sayer. He had just installed his life-size replica of *T rex* on the lawn in front of the resort. He invited Jo and I to join him for lunch with his wife and some executive staff in the boardroom, during which he outlined his intention to build the *Titanic II* and complete that fateful maiden voyage, steaming into New York. He dazzled us with plans and drawings of the ship, identical in almost every way to the original but with modern safety and propulsion systems.

Clive then said he wanted to take me around the world to help promote the venture and promised us a berth on the first journey. I was intrigued by the whole concept and we began negotiations with his close staff, who seemed to think such ambitions were just part of their boss's personality. Glenn Shorrock and band were to be the entertainment at three dinners to be held in Macau, New York and London. How could I refuse? Not only was I thrilled to be part of the impressive but very ambitious project but the deal he was offering was too generous to refuse.

The first stop on this tour in early 2013 was Macau at the 3000-room Venetian hotel and casino. The whole event was covered in the *Titanic II* promotional material; a video presentation was played in the lobby and dinner was served to 600 people; the exact eleven-course menu served on the first (and last) voyage.

New York came next. The venue was the USS *Intrepid* a decommissioned aircraft carrier now permanently moored on the Hudson River and the centrepoint of a museum. The now empty hanger beneath the flight desk is used as an event venue and that's where the Clive show happened. We were given little assistance in setting up for our sound check, the New York

teamster union were in no mood for sensitive Aussie musicians, until we ran through 'Reminiscing' and heads began to turn when they realised who I was. 'That's the guy ...' someone shouted, and instantly they couldn't do enough for us. It was a telling moment and it was a similar reaction from guests wanting to meet me and get 'selfies' as I worked the room.

It was great to get to London next; Jo and I always feel comfortable there. This time we were housed at the Royal Kensington Hotel in Knightsbridge, next to the Kensington Palace and Gardens. Some of the band went on a pilgrimage to Abbey Road but Jo and I caught up with family and friends and enjoyed walks in the crisp, sunny winter air.

Clive had secured the lobby of the Natural History Museum for the next function. The logistics were challenging. We had to wait until 5 pm closing before a huge team built a ballroom around the famous dinosaur skeleton, with table seating for about 400 guests (an impressive feat!). We were welcomed there, as there were a lot of Australians present including ex-South Australia Premier Mike Rann, then the Australian High Commissioner, and fan.

Titanic II was to be built along with four iron-ore bulk carriers, the cost being absorbed by the Chinese. Unfortunately, Clive's romantic dream succumbed to the harsh realities in the risky high-end of life in the financial world. I have a certain amount of sympathy for the effort made by him and his long-suffering staff to realise what would have been an amazing adventure. Alas, I doubt it will ever be built.

******

Of course, being in a band means you get to travel. The French Quarter of New Orleans is a living, breathing museum of music, and it is a must-visit for anyone interested in the evolution of America's finest export. To walk down Bourbon Street on a hot

With the great Dennis Lillee in the late 1970s, discussing how to bat! 'DK' presented me a signed bat at the height of the World Series Cricket rebel series and he and Rod Marsh came to lunch at the Anchorage some years later. I am a cricket fan and, by the look on my face, rather enthralled!

summer's night with a Hurricane cocktail in one hand hearing 'Walkin' To New Orleans' by Fats Domino is one of life's true rewards.

The Australian Consulate in Abu Dhabi hold a Christmas concert party every year and I was booked there in 2013. It took place on the shores of the Gulf, just across for the Hilton where we stayed for four days. The show was well received but the sightseeing overshadowed the event. We were shown around by an attaché and the highlights included a visit to the Golden Mosque, a monument of staggering beauty. From the sublime, we then spent an afternoon at Ferrari World at the Grand Prix circuit. Right up my alley! The roller-coaster boasted to be the world's fastest and I believe it – the acceleration was that of a Formula One car.

Some places in Australia become very familiar but there are always fresh venues. The Kimberley is the most spectacular part of the country we've been in and of course Uluru is up there as well. We've done the top end a few times: Darwin to Broome in a Brits campervan along the bitumen; once, the other outback way on the Gibb River Road via El Questro and Emma Gorge with our friends Gael (McKay) and her husband Francesco Boglione and their children; and another time to Cape Leveque, three hours north of Broome, to stay in beautiful safari tents for a week.

The colours there are unforgettable; the red earth against the blue sky, the white sand and turquoise sea. We had the best lunch of our life there. Mud crabs caught by our Aboriginal hosts (who own the land and co-manage the resort) cooked in a big, battered drum on the beach, dipping the sweet, fleshy claws in the seawater, washing them down with blizzardly cold beer and wine – heaven! It's a fun drive there and back too, along a red track with ruts so deep you don't have to steer! Needless to say, it comes highly recommended.

Lizard Island on the North Queensland Barrier Reef and, more recently, Albany in Western Australia, have been a treat. Albany is south of Perth, with Margaret River halfway along to refresh oneself. Yes, this big country is hard to beat. Of course, places overseas have treated us well also. South-East Asia, Hong Kong, China, Europe and the US of A were very accommodating professionally and personally.

About twenty years ago, Brian Cadd and I were invited to the Port Moresby Jazz and Blues Festival. 'The what?' was our first reaction and it proved to be an unforgettable, rough gig. We were sometimes in fear of our lives! Things were pretty lawless back then and our hotel was a walled, barbwire compound. Brian and I tried our best to pretend we were jazz musicians, playing 'A Little Ray Of Sunshine' in 5/4 time. I think we got away with it!

Cadd and I were also favourites of the Australian Association of Hong Kong, which is made up largely of Qantas air crew and ex-pats. Great hotel, great food and great people; we would go out on junks to nearby fishing islands and Jo would shop!

Brian and I did the Big Red Bash a couple of years ago. We took our Sharky & the Caddman show to 10,000 people in the middle of outback Australia, sharing the bill over three days with Christine Anu, Shane Howard and Russell Morris. The Bash is presented each year at the base of Big Red, reputably the tallest sand dune in the country. Unfortunately, flooding rains washed that out and the show went on at the home of the Birdsville races. I'd do it again in a New York minute, such fun even with the dodgy air travel. Our plane broke down in Mount Isa and we had to stay an extra night but I don't remember much of that!

******

My touring band was now largely Melbourne-based although I was in Sydney, but I enjoyed working with Stewart Wilkinson, Pip Joyce, Jason Vorherr, Dave Beck and Gary Young and we travelled all over the country together. The term 'unplugged' was

used at the time. I embraced the concept; acoustic music has always appealed to me and the lower volume level was also attractive. So Los Trios Taragos was born, meaning we could play intimate venues, as Glenn, Stew, Pip and Dave all packed neatly into a rented Tarago. We produced an acoustic album for Mushroom's Liberation label, recorded at Jo Camilleri's Woodstock Studio in Balaclava Road, Melbourne. The album was presented as one of their Liberation Blue series in a fashionable cardboard fold-out cover complete with insert written eloquently by an old friend and celebrated radio voice, Barry Bissell. The tracks became the centre of our acoustic show and the cardboard version is now a proverbial 'collector's item'. Angus Birchall played drums on the record as Dave Beck was not available. Dave had started a lovely new family with two young daughters and opted for the regular income in the 'pit' of orchestras of musicals.

Availability has always been an issue for me and my live work since I have been a solo artist. I have my go-to guys both in Melbourne and here in Sydney; unfortunately, a lot of them are also the go-to guys for my fellow colleagues like Ross Wilson, Joe Camilleri, Darryl Braithwaite and Leo Sayer, but we all seem to

Standing alongside trumpeter James Morrison meeting Princess Anne at a Prince's Trust Charity Ball in London in 1989 (John Farnham and Renée Geyer were also on the bill).

make it work. Oz rock is blessed these days with fine professional people who are now able to afford a good lifestyle, as opposed to the bad ol' Chiko Roll days. 'Farnsy' and 'Barnsy', however, are able to command exclusivity from their musos, and good luck to them. John Paul Young and Wendy Matthews also prefer to have their own people around them all the time.

John Farnham is a freak; he can go higher, faster and longer than anyone else, and is certainly the most dynamic singer Australia has produced. As Australia's King of Pop, he wanted to brush off that persona. When he joined LRB he respected the work I had put into the band and carried that on for a few years and I supported him in that. John was a lot like me in that he also wanted to be liked on stage and was very demonstrative with the audience. His success with *Whispering Jack* put him in the most rarefied position of being able to tour at will across Australia.

I like Jimmy Barnes a lot. When we toured together with *Long Way To The Top*, he wanted to do a duet with me and suggested 'Needle In A Haystack' because he wanted to sing the 'she-doo wops' in that distinctive gravel voice of his and ended up singing a Nat King Cole duet. Go figure!. I quickly learned not to be in the same room as him when he was warming up before a show – it's like standing beside the engine of small jet!

Having your own touring band gives you the luxury to change repertoire and have exclusivity but having many players around the country who know your show gives you more work and keeps you on your toes. Flexibility is necessary in this business and that's why I wear elastic pants!

Seriously, I owe so much to my side men over the years who have presented my music so well and given me great service. This includes my Sydney band as well as my 'Wrecking Crew': the wonderful Paul Gray, John Bettison, Rex Goh, Paul Berton, Gordon Rytmeister, Emile Nelson, Bill Risby and Mick Skelton.

They are all stars in their own right.

CHAPTER 20

Le Grand Tour

I often find myself contemplating my failings or learnings over the seven-plus decades of my life. As it so often happens, when I am awake in the middle of the night and can't sleep, I find it a good time for self-examination. I have often been criticised for not showing my emotions, which is an emotion in itself, and not expressing my feelings. I think detachment from emotion is a good thing sometimes but callousness and a lack of charity is not.

Of all the nicknames I have been given the one that annoys me is 'Mr Grumpy' but I accept that I do have a negativity inherited from my family. I like to think I'm more of a pragmatic realist with an inquisitive sense of humour! Did I mention occasional selfishness and drunkenness?

'Ah, sweet mystery of life at last I've found you ...'

Am I a happy person? I'm not unhappy but I get down on myself sometimes. I'm healthy, relatively speaking. Since moving to Double Bay, I've been attending gym sessions as regularly as possible but I'm in my seventies now and I know that forty years ago I was at the absolute top of my game. I go through periods now where I struggle to retain my confidence but I find meditation helps.

I get anxious now before a gig – the guy once voted most likely to fall asleep five minutes before going on stage – but I relax after a couple of songs. I was invited by Tennis Australia to sing the national anthem at the Australian Open Tennis championship at

With Jo at Cape Leveque on the Dampier Peninsula near Broome, WA, one of our favourite destinations in the world. I love the sunset colours in this photo and the fact that we are standing underneath the 'eagle rock' (or is it a penguin?)

the Rod Laver Arena, entirely alone and with no accompaniment. When 16,000 people rose to their feet and I began my rendition of *Advance Australia Fair* I immediately became aware that I was being televised worldwide as well. To my horror my left buttock began to twitch and shake and I imagined it being noticed by the audience behind me and internationally on TV!

My left side joined in and then my microphone began to shake, quickly I grasped it with my other hand but soon my whole body felt like I was performing the St Vitus dance! I got through unscathed, and probably unnoticed, but it was a telling moment for me. It awakened in me a nervousness that was previously absent and has occurred frequently over the past decade or so.

I've learned to enjoy the here and now, which is pretty bloody good! I take every day as it comes; when I wake in the morning I check that everything is still working and that I can stand upright!

I'm the longevity guy. My work ethic hasn't been Olympic but I've managed to run the race at my pace. I've had a few wins but have always been around the placings. I've had a lot more staying power than many of my music colleagues too: I could drink more, smoke more and stay up longer than most!

Life is full, work is plentiful and my voice has stayed strong along with my physical condition. People are always saying that I don't look my age so I suppose I'm having a good life. Vanity and appearance are good arbiters of that; I often joke that's why there are no mirrors in my home!

I didn't know what I wanted to do with my life until music came along. I gained success with the little amount of effort and talent that I have. If I hadn't made it as a singer I think I would have made a good A&R man in the record business but there is no record business anymore so now I just offer my opinions like everybody else.

I love performing and I like the recognition that I get that I'm a good singer. I think I'm much better than a lot of people give

'I am Caesar' snapped by Jo while clowning around in the Greek Isles.

me credit for. I have a distinctive pop voice and I pride myself on the fact that people can understand what I sing and what I mean.

I have recorded two albums this century, *Meanwhile* in 2007 and *Rise Again* in 2016, and a CD/DVD compilation *45 Years Of Song* (2010). I get frustrated that my music doesn't get played on air any more – the people who run radio today are not music fans, they're business people – or reviewed in the papers, but my audience have remained loyal and I still love to perform live.

Today, I'm not so driven to be successful all over again. I've said it many times over the years but I started small in the music business and am resigned to the fact that I will most likely finish small.

My career is still my life, and vice versa, and they are rarely separate. When opportunities have come my way, I've accepted most of them with mostly good results, but you win some and you lose some and I've probably wasted a few by not caring too much. The decisions I've made have been reached largely from my own search for pleasure and happiness but sometimes the decisions are made for me and I'll go along for the ride. I guess the point I'm trying to make is little has been planned, what has happened has happened and I've got on with it and enjoyed it.

Regrets, I've had a few, but then again …

I regret not being able to play a virtuous instrument – a guitar, a violin, a piano. I am still astounded by the subtlety and nuances of classical music; the ability of the great masters to hear a symphony in their head and write it down on paper. I can envisage a sound or melody in my head but it's hard to get it down on paper, to put the notes down in the right place as it were.

In saying that, I suppose my music will be played long after I've gone and I'm pleased with that. I have to grit my teeth sometimes because of all the LRB baggage but I'm quite happy that out of the many songs LRB is known for, some are mine: 'Cool Change', 'Help Is On Its Way' and 'Home On A Monday'. Graeham's 'Reminiscing' isn't a bad legacy song to have either but I prefer others. 'It's A Long Way There' is more indicative of the LRB sound.

I have always described myself as a lucky man; lucky to have been born with a sense of humour and fairness and to have been blessed with a good singing voice. Money has never been a problem for me; I like having it, and somehow, I've had enough of it when it was needed, depending of course on what my needs have been. I've also managed happily without it.

My social life today largely centres on my devoted wife Jo, who has both embraced and enhanced all the people in our life. Jo and I have been together since 1975 and she is a huge part of my life and success during these past years. Jo was a free spirit when we met who had travelled the world and was undecided

Petersham House, in Richmond, Surrey; the home of our friends Francesco and Gael Boglione.

Jo and I at a wedding in Mexico, 2008.

about her future with a musician with little money, as she puts it, but we gave it a shot and we've had a long and largely happy journey together. She has been a good wife and a great friend. I know she would have loved to have been a mother, as I would have loved to be a father to her children, but it was not meant to be. Life's been very hectic and I haven't been responsible for anyone else except myself and I've only done a 50/50 job at that at times.

So, I'm the end of the Shorrock line. However, there are numerous offspring in our lives for Jo to dote upon and we have watched them grow into adulthood.

We both love visiting our friends overseas and go to Europe regularly. Gael Boglione and Jo are still close friends and we join the Bogliones often on holidays. Francesco is a fine skier (as a young man he was close to Olympic standard) and they have built a beautiful lodge near Sestriere on the Italian border. It is unique to that area as it was designed and built in Canada from disused Redwood logs, dismantled, shipped, and reconstructed by the Canadians on site in Monte de la Luna. It's a joy to ski across the border into France, have a croissant and coffee and be back for lunch in a classic mountain trattoria for lunch in Italy.

It's not too shabby staying with them at home in London

either; they live in a significant Georgian House on the edge of Richmond Park on the Thames. Over the years they secured a somewhat dilapidated neighbouring nursery and have transformed it into the most fabulous nursery and restaurant, Petersham Nurseries, which has become the go-to place for the wealthy and fashionable.

Suffice to say my career has afforded me a lifestyle I had not imagined and still don't take for granted.

In 2008, we were invited to the wedding of two very dear friends in Mexico, Louise de Teliga and C.B. Harding. That wonderful event became an excuse for a round-the-world trip that we christened 'Le Grand Tour'. We arrived in LA and had a couple of nights there before we flew down to Porta Vallarta on the Pacific coast of Mexico. The wedding was beautiful; a mariachi band serenaded the handsome couple and I did the same at the reception, to the surprise of their American guests who recognised my songs.

Jo in Havana … have a cigar!

We had always wanted to visit Cuba and were excited when
we touched down in Havana after a short flight from Cancun.
On finding our accommodation had been screwed up, we
were upgraded to a suite in the Park Central Hotel and given a
complimentary bottle of Havana Club dark rum. It went down
nicely and has become a personal favourite. Walking around this
city was fascinating, just like the travelogues – shabby chic began
here! We sheltered from a storm in a bar and came across a trio
called Sol de Soi a marimba-led funky salsa group who held our
attention long after the storm had passed. They sat with us in
between sets and we shared our experiences with a few mojitos.

There were no direct flights into the US from Cuba, the
diplomatic standoff being still in place (it was not so wise to
have Cuba on your passport in those days either). So, we did
a short overnight backtrack to Cancun, Mexico and then on to
New York. Despite the heat I enjoyed our time in New York,
having on previous visits felt the energy a little overpowering.

Our week ended with a walk over the Brooklyn Bridge and a visit to Ground Zero to pay our respects to the victims of the September 11 attacks. Very moving.

On to Spain, and to Bilbao via Madrid; a visit to a smaller gallery to view Peter Blake work (he is famous for the *Sgt. Pepper's* album cover) completed our stay there. We left on the AVE, the extremely fast train to Madrid; amazing to hurtle through the Aussie-like terrain at 270 kilometres per hour eating caviar canapes chased down with vodka. Ah well, someone has to do it!

In Madrid on Sunday morning, we continued our art odyssey and walked to the Museo Reina Sofia in a modest side street. We were blown away with the treasures within: Miró, Dali, Picasso including *Guernica* – an amazing collection.

We then took a short flight back to Madrid before continuing on to Marrakech to spend a week in Morocco. Our last day there was probably one too many as the heat was getting to us and we hid from it in the relative respite of our charming room. It was the night of my sixty-fourth birthday and I was given a delicious home-cooked meal by our French hosts, along with a surprise cake and champagne.

Houghton Hall, Norfolk, the family home of our host David, the 7th Marquess of Cholmondeley and the Earl of Rocksavage.

'Will you still need me, will you still feed me when I'm sixty-four?'

Our flight to Heathrow was via Madrid, where my newly acquired duty-free bottle of Havana Club was confiscated. I was furious and tried to negotiate with customs but had to hand it over. I'm sure they enjoyed it.

We were welcomed back in Petersham House by Gael and Francesco and were invited to spend a weekend at a stunning 9000-acre property and had a glimpse into the English aristocratic life. The 7th Marquess of Cholmondeley David Rocksavage (what a great name!) was a wonderful host without airs and graces. Needless to say, we wallowed in his hospitality and marvelled at his lifestyle, just down the road from Sandringham House owned by his godmother, the Queen.

We roamed tipsily after dinner under a magical moon that night and, after a huge country breakfast of homemade sausages, continued through lunch and dinner while enjoying the British Grand Prix and the Wimbledon men's final (which went on for five sets and was still going when we arrived back in London). A fitting finale to Le Grand Tour.

******

Jo and I have seen a lot of the world together and there are still places on our list but not in a bucket!

I'm sometimes asked which am I, English or Australian? I feel I'm both but more than anything I'm an Adelaidean. Adelaide may not be the first city that comes to mind when you mention Australia to people around the world but I love it there and have kept a close connection over the years.

In October 2014, I was inducted into the South Australian Music Hall of Fame alongside Bon Scott's former band Fraternity. Recently I reaffirmed my Adelaide heritage with a show that I devised with the encouragement and help of Rob Pippan, a fan

who has become a good friend, and who has joined me on guitar on many occasions over the years and has led from the front.

The show was well received as part of the Fringe Festival. We thought it would be a good idea to revisit my early days in Elizabeth where I spent my formative years so I invited my first besties Paddy McCartney and Mike Sykes to join me on stage to talk and laugh and sing about our early forays into the world of music etc. I think they enjoyed it but I was conscious that I was throwing them into an environment that is no longer theirs, although it was good to rekindle our bond and friendship again.

I hope they didn't feel too exploited by my somewhat selfish reasons for asking them to be part of the show but they were an important part of my life.

I'm an Australian when I'm overseas although I'm wary of being too jingoistic or 'true blue' Aussie at home. I like to think of myself as a world citizen and support unity rather than parochialism. If I had my way I would do away with borders but

I love this photo of Jo in Mexico, a pensive mood and a latte in hand.

I know I'm only dreaming ('but I'm not the only one', as John Lennon once sang).

I was lucky to have been part of a cultural revolution in music and the arts and experienced the great leap forward for humankind. I believe we still need to show more 'humankindness'. At this time of writing this world of ours us in so much misery and the suffering of so many can sometimes overwhelm me and angers me. Why do we have to put up with leaders who are unsuitable to lead and why do we follow them? This insatiable quest for more financial growth and accumulation of wealth only favours the already wealthy and never seems to benefit the needy.

I have long taken an interest in the future of our planet and species but from a more cosmic parameter. We should be preparing for life in 100 to 500 years from now, not the shortsighted vision of ten to twenty years ahead that is argued now. I'm known as being a bit of a doomsday prophet but maybe the barn door has already closed and we are headed for disaster. Perhaps we could slow down that inevitability?

As a fellow member of humanity, as such, I have concerns for our future as a species. We are quick to point out our differences and place unnecessary divisions between us but it's often the differences that attract us to each other. The inner self is much more interesting than the outer image. But if I was to come to my own conclusion it would be this: I am no different than you.

As I said at the beginning, my main reason for writing this book was to let you get to know the real me (having always described 'me' as being my favourite subject). As Bette Midler once said, if I remember correctly, 'That's enough about me. Let's talk about *you*! What do *you* think of my new album?'

Epilogue

Ok it's time to put this baby to bed now. I dilly-dallied at the beginning and now I'm doing the same at the end, for a couple of reasons I might add. I feel I've said enough about me and the subject is wearing thin, something that my physique is doing now along with the rest of my faculties!

Recently, we spent Christmas with my 97-year-old mother and my sister's family, doing a bit of stocktaking and discussing the 'family fortunes' which have improved of late. A decade ago, my cousin Geoffrey alerted me to a suspicion he had regarding his brother Phillip's handling of our Aunty Madeline's will. She and her late husband, our Uncle John, had bought a significant parcel of Kentish countryside just outside Whitstable which we knew she had apportioned amongst us.

Elder brother Phillip had stayed close to Aunt Mad in her final years and when the developers came knocking his eyes must have lit up. Geoffrey said his brother was now claiming that our aunt had left it all to him. So began an ugly, six-year-long battle, brother against brother, in which I played a supporting part, which ended in a High Court ruling in our favour. We struck a deal which secured my mother's comfort in her old age, along with Lynda and her family. Geoff and I also got our just desserts but Phillip? Not so much. He's dropped off the family radar, deservedly so.

I know my mum misses my father Harry too much to go on

My wife Jo and I, in our fifth decade together now.
(Courtesy Simon Kenny)

much longer without him. She is tired and a little lonely, as many of her friends and neighbours have passed on. She has been a supportive mother to me and I think has enjoyed my career vicariously, with a smattering of envy and indeed some criticism. She has loved my sister Lynda and I unconditionally and we are both products of that love.

Lynda has stayed close and looked after Mum in recent years and has still managed to be a great mother and now grandmother herself. Thank you, sis.

The person that knows me best is of course Jo. I've done my bit but she has contributed much more to our relationship and deserves her own success, which she has in her dealings with humanity in general and within the life that we have fashioned together. We make a good team; she forgives and I forget.

So, I'm coming to the end now ... not of my life but of ducking the question posed by the title of this book. Now, where was I? I know where I've been and now ponder where to in the future. Suffice to say, I'll keep on keeping on. I love to sing and there are still so many songs to visit and revisit in the years ahead. Most of my life is described in those songs.

Thanks for the melodies, sorry, memories.

Discography

Glenn Shorrock: Selected Discography (1965–2016)

* songs written by Glenn Shorrock

The Twilights
(1965–69)

SINGLES

I'll Be Where You Are * / I Don't Know Where The Wind Will Blow Me * * (Columbia DO 4582) June 1965 * with Terry Britten, * * with Peter Brideoake

Come On Home / Wanted To Sell (Columbia DO 4610) 1965

If She Finds Out / John Hardy (Columbia DO 4658) 1966

Baby Let Me Take You Home / You've Really Got A Hold On Me (Columbia DO 4685) 1966

Bad Boy / It's Dark (Columbia DO 4698) 1966

Needle In A Haystack / I Won't Be The Same Without Her (Columbia DO 4717) 1966

You Got Soul / Yes I Will (Columbia DO 4742) 1966

What's Wrong With The Way I Live / 9.50 (Columbia DO 4764) 1967

Young Girl / Time & Motion Study Man (Columbia DO 4787) 1967

Cathy Come Home / The Way They Play (Columbia DO 5030) 1967

Bowling Brings Out The Swinger in You / Bowling Brings Out The Swinger in You (instrumental version) (EMI Custom PRS 1736, promotional single) 1967

Always / What A Silly Thing To Do (Columbia DO 8361) 1968

Tell Me Goodbye / Comin' On Down (Columbia DO 8448) 1968

Sand in the Sandwiches / Lotus (Columbia DO 8602) 1968

2,000 Weeks / Bargain Day (Columbia DO 8711) 1969

EPs

Bad Boy
(Columbia SEGO-70129) 1966

I'll Be Where You Are * with Terry Britten / If She Finds Out / Baby, Let Me Take You Home / Bad Boy

Needle In A Haystack
(Columbia SEGO-70139) 1967

Needle In A Haystack / What's Wrong With The Way I Live / 9.50 / Young Girl

Always
(Columbia SEGO-70161) 1968

You Got Soul / The Way They Play / Cathy, Come Home / Always

LPs

The Twilights
(Columbia 33OSX-7779) 1966

Sorry, She's Mine
La La La Lies
It's Dark
Diddy Wa Diddy
Long Life
Needle In A Haystack
You've Got Soul
Yes I Will
I'm Not Talkin'
Let Me Go
Lucky Man
Satisfaction

Once Upon A Twilight
(Columbia SCXO-7870) 1968

Once Upon A Twilight
What A Silly Thing To Do
Bessemae
Stop The World For A Day
Mr. Nice
Take Action
Blue Roundabout

Devendra
Found To Be Thrown Away
Tomorrow Is Today
Cocky Song
Paternosta Row

Axiom
(1969–71)

SINGLES

Arkansas Grass / Samantha
(Parlophone, A-8909) 1969

A Little Ray Of Sunshine /
Ford's Bridge (Parlophone,
A-9070) 1970

Father Confessor / Time and
Time Again (Warner Bros, 6134)
1970

My Baby's Gone / Hold The
Phone (Warner Bros, 8021) 1971

Fool's Gold / Yesterday, Today
And Tomorrow (Parlophone,
A-9421) 1971

EP

The Axiom Hits
(Warner Bros, EPW 201) 1972

Father Confessor /A Little Ray
Of Sunshine / My Baby's Gone /
Time And Time Again

LPs

Fool's Gold
(Parlophone, PCSO.7561) 1970

Arkansas Grass
Baby Bear
Ford's Bridge
Samantha
Take It Or Leave It
A Little Ray Of Sunshine
Yesterday, Today And Tomorrow
Mansfield Hotel
Can't Let Go Of This Feeling
Country Pickin'
Once A Month Country
Race Day

Fool's Gold
Who Am I Gonna See?

If Only …
(Warner Bros, WS-3009) 1971

Father Confessor
Hold The Phone
Sailing Ships
Talking About It
My Baby's Gone
Time And Time Again
Longest Day
Georgia By Morning
Matter Of Time
A Little Ray Of Sunshine

Solo Years 1
(1971–75)

SINGLES

Purple Umbrella / Petunia
(MAM, MAM 36) (released
as Andre L'Escargot and His
Society Syncopaters) 1971

Let's Get The Band Together /
Contemporary Cave Man
(MAM, MAM 46) * both Glenn
Shorrock, 1971

Rock And Roll Lullaby / When
God Plays His Guitar * (MAM,
MAM 65) , 1972

Daydream Sunday / I Have Seen
The Universe (Playboy Records,
P 6027)

Esperanto
(1973–74)

SINGLES

Busy Doing Nothing / Move
Away (A&M Records 12 984 AT)
* both with Raymond Vincent,
1973

Statue Of Liberty * / Gypsy
(A&M Records 1478-S
promotional)

LPs

Esperanto Rock Orchestra
(A&M Records 68175) 1973

On Down The Road *
with Raymond Vincent
Never Again
Perhaps One Day
Statue Of Liberty *
Gypsy
Seine City *
with Raymond Vincent
Roses
Move Away *
with Raymond Vincent

Danse Macabre
(A&M Records 71041974) 1974

The Journey
The Castle * with Raymond
Vincent/Bruno Libert
The Duel
The Cloister * with Raymond
Vincent/Bruno Libert
The Decision
The Prisoner *
with Raymond Vincent
Danse Macabre

Little River Band
(1975–82 and
1986–1995)

SINGLES

Curiosity (Killed the Cat) / I Just
Don't Get The Feeling Anymore
(EMI, EMI-10900) 1975

Emma / Love Is A Feeling (EMI,
EMI-11003) 1975

It's a Long Way There / Time to
Fly (EMI, EMI -11292) 1975

I'll Always Call Your Name /
The Man in Black (EMI, EMI-
2591) 1975 *

Everyday of My Life / Days on
the Road (EMI, EMI-11116)

Help Is On Its Way * / Changed And Different * (EMI, EMI-11405)

Witchery / LA In The Sunshine * (EMI, EMI-11491) * with David Briggs

Home On A Monday * / Raelene Raelene (EMI, EMI-11522) 1977

Happy Anniversary / Changed And Different (Harvest, 4524) 1977

Shut Down Turn Off * / Days on the Road (Live) (EMI – EMI-11691) 1978

Reminiscing / Take Me Home (EMI, EMI-11738) 1978

Lady / Happy Anniversary (EMI, EMI-11800) 1978

Lonesome Loser / Another Runway (Capitol, CP-11972) 1979

Cool Change * / Middle Man (Capitol, 4789) 1979

Long Jumping Jeweller * / I Don't Worry Anymore (Capitol, CP-407) 1980

The Night Owls / Suicide Boulevard (Capitol, CP-570) 1981

Take It Easy On Me / Orbit Zero * (Capitol, A-5057) 1981

Man on Your Mind / Love Will Survive (Capitol, CP-633 1982) 1981 * with Kerryn Tolhurst

Love is a Bridge / Inside Story (MCA Records, 7-53291) 1988

Son of a Famous Man / Lyin' Eyes/Take It Easy (WEA, 7-10013) 1988

Soul Searching * / Great Unknown * * (MCA, 7-57841) 1988 * with Peter Beckett, * * with John Boylan

If I Get Lucky / Piece of My Heart (MCA, 7-53767) 1990

LPs

Little River Band
(EMI, ST-11512) 1975

It's A Long Way There
Curiosity (Killed The Cat)
Meanwhile *
My Lady And Me
I'll Always Call Your Name
Emma *
The Man In Black *
Statue Of Liberty *
I Know It

After Hours
(EMI, EMC 125) 1976

Days On The Road
Every Day Of My Life
Broke Again
Seine City *
Another Runway
Bourbon Street
Sweet Old Fashioned Man *
Take Me Home
Country Girls

Diamantina Cocktail
(EMI, EMC.2575) 1977

Help Is On Its Way *
The Drifter
L. A. In The Sunshine * with David Briggs
The Inner Light
Witchery
Home On A Monday * with Beeb Birtles
Happy Anniversary
Raelene, Raelene
Changed And Different

Sleeper Catcher
(EMI, EMA 786) 1978

Fall From Paradise
Lady
Red-Headed Wildflower
Light Of Day
So Many Paths * with Idris Jones
Reminiscing

Sanity's Side * with Charles Dawes
Shut Down, Turn Off *
One For The Road

First Under the Wire
(Capitol, ST.11954) 1979

Lonesome Loser
The Rumour *
By My Side
Cool Change *
It's Not A Wonder
Hard Life (Prelude)
Hard Life
Middle Man
Man on the Run
Mistress of Mine

Time Exposure
(Capitol, 1C 064-400 042) 1981

The Night Owls
Man On Your Mind * with Kerryn Tolhurst
Take It Easy On Me
Ballerina
Love Will Survive
Full Circle
Just Say That You Love Me
Suicide Boulevard
Orbit Zero * with Terry Bradford
Don't Let the Needle Win
Guiding Light

Too Late to Load
(EMI, CDP 791693) 1988

When Will I Be Loved
"D"
Gunslinger *
Please Don't Ask Me
The Shut Out
One Day
Love Letters
Stormy Surrender
What Ya Thinka Me
Tender Betrayal
The Butterfly (instrumental)
Chip Off The Old Block *

Monsoon
(MCA, MCAD-42193) 1988

It's Cold Out Tonight

Parallel Lines *
with J.C. Crowley

Love is a Bridge

The Rhythm King

Face in the Crowd

A Cruel Madness

Inside Story

Son of a Famous Man

Soul Searching *
with Peter Beckett

Great Unknown *
with John Boylan

Shadow in the Rain

Get Lucky
(MCA, 2292-57164-1) 1990

If I Get Lucky

There's Not Another You

Second Wind

Every Time I Turn Around

I Dream Alone *
with Derek Pellicci

Time and Eternity

Two Emotions

As Long as I'm Alive

The One That Got Away

Listen to Your Heart

Solo Years 2
(1982–86, 1996–2018)

SINGLES

Dream Lover / Spin Me 'Round
(EMI, EMI-11923) 1979

Rock 'n' Roll Soldier * * / The
Duchess Is Returning * (Capitol
Records, CP-834) 1982 * * with
Terry Bradford

Villain Of The Peace / Villain
Of The Peace (Capitol Records,
B-5281 promotional) 1983 *
with Terry Bradford

Don't Girls Get Lonely / Do It
Anyway * (Capitol Records,
ECS-17396) 1983 * with Kerryn
Tolhurst

American Flyers / The Duchess
Is Returning * (Capitol Records,
CP-1802) 1986

LPs

Villain Of The Peace
(Capitol Records, ST-12222) 1982

Rock 'n' Roll Soldier *
with Terry Bradford

Secrets * with Jo Shorrock

Summer In The City

Onwards And Upwards *
with John Boylan

A Cry In A Jungle Bar *
with John Boylan

Villain Of The Peace *

Angry Words

Martinique

Do It Anyway *
with Kerryn Tolhurst

Will You Stand With Me? *

Spin Me 'Round
(Streetwise Music Group, SW20016)
2000

Spin Me 'Round *

Hard Bargain * with Brian Cadd

Walk Away

At The Mercy Of The Sea

When You Love Someone

Living Beyond Our Dreams

Dixie Wire

Just Might Be The First *

Angry Words

Will You Stand With Me? *

Meanwhile … Acoustically
(Liberation Blue, BLUE146.5) 2007

Will You Stand With Me? *

Meanwhile *

Home On A Monday *
with Beeb Birtles

Help Is On Its Way *

Cool Change *

Emma *

Reminiscing

Rock 'n' Roll Soldier *
with Terry Bradford

Needle In A Haystack

Soul Searching *
with Peter Beckett

So Many Paths * with Jones

Unrequited Love *
with J.C. Crowley

Dream Lover

Seine City *

Rise Again
(Social Family Records SFR0053)
2016

Hear My Voice *

The Wood And The Wire

Rise Again

Emperors Clothes *

Stick up Your Finger *

Trouble

Slice of Heaven

Make a Difference

Candlelight Moon

10

Blissful Oblivion

Compilations

**Glenn Shorrock:
The First 20 Years**
(EMI, 0777 7 46306 8 9) originally
1985, released on CD 1996

The Twilights –

Needle In A Haystack

Bad Boy

If She Finds Out

9.50

Young Girl

What's Wrong With The Way
I Live?

Cathy Come Home

My Generation

Axiom –

Ford's Bridge

Fool's Gold
Arkansas Grass
A Little Ray Of Sunshine
My Baby's Gone

Little River Band –

Cool Change *
Home On A Monday
Shut Down, Turn Off *
Help Is On Its Way *
Man On Your Mind
Long Jumping Jeweller

Glenn Shorrock –

Rock 'n' Roll Lullaby
Let's Get The Band Together
Statue Of Liberty
Seine City
When Will I Be Loved?
Goin' Back (with Renée Geyer)
We're Coming To Get You!
(with the Bushwackers)
Paperback Writer
Dream Lover
Restless
Don't Girls Get Lonely?
Big Smoke
Will You Stand With Me?
The Duchess Is Returning
Rock 'n' Roll Soldier

With *Renée Geyer*

Goin' Back / (We Got
The Makings Of A) Fever
(Mushroom, K-9001) 1983

With *The Bushwackers*

We're Coming To Get You /
We're Coming To Get You
(Instrumental) (EMI, EMI-1059)
1983

With *Brian Cadd* (as Blazing Salads)

A Little Ray Of Sunshine
/ Life Of Brian * (EMI, 8740272)
1992 * with Brian Cadd

When It All Comes Down /
Blazing Salad Cream / Love
Drives A Hard Bargain (EMI,
EMI- 8740192) 1993 * with
Brian Cadd

Out Of Time / Blazing Salad
Cream * / My Own Way Home
* (Blue Martin Records, BLM
339039-2) 1994 * with Brian
Cadd

LP

Blazing Salads
(EMI, EMI-7814662) 1993

When The Words Come *
with Brian Cadd
Shake The Hand *
with Brian Cadd
When It All Comes Down *
with Brian Cadd
De-Emphasize *
with Brian Cadd
Tear Down The Barricades
A Little Ray Of Sunshine
Between The Lines *
with Brian Cadd
Out Of Time
Life Of Brian * with Brian Cadd
My Own Way Home *
with Brian Cadd
(The Angel of the Fjord and
the Boy from) Capricorn *
with Brian Cadd

**The Story of Sharky
& the Caddman**
(Fanfare Classic, FANFARE122) 2013

Tear Down The Barricades
Angry Words
Hate And Love
Arkansas Grass

A Little Ray Of Sunshine
My Baby's Gone
Axiom Medley: Sailing Ships /
Mansfield Hotel / Fool's Gold /
Ford's Bridge
Mama Don't Dance
Home On A Monday *
with Beeb Birtles
Let Go
Reminiscing
Don't You Know It's Magic
Help Is On It's Way *
Ginger Man
Cool Change *

With *Birtles Shorrock Goble*

LP

Full Circle
(Universal Music Australia, 9811807)
2003

Full Circle
It's A Long Way There
Man On Your Mind *
with Kerryn Tolhurst
Curiosity (Killed The Cat)
Everyday Of My Life
Happy Anniversary
Prelude In A Minor
Mistress Of Mine
Lady
Take It Easy On Me
The Night Owls
The Other Guy
Seine City *
Home On A Monday *
with Beeb Birtles
Reminiscing
Help Is On Its Way *
Cool Change *
Lonesome Loser

Acknowledgements

To publisher Alan Whiticker and all the hard-working team at New Holland Publishers.

Thank you to John Boylan, the 'Jimmy Stewart' of the record business and Sir George Martin, 'that other producer'.

To all the photographers featured in this book, known and unknown, but especially Geoff Hales, Simon Kenny, Bob King and Tony Mott. My sincere gratitude.

And to all the people I've worked with over the years, on and off the bandstand (I know where you live).

Many thanks to all the hotel, airline and other service people who have helped me too ... we're all in the same industry really.

To the Sydney Swans, my favourite football team.

To mum Joyce and sister Lynda and her family.

To Kelly, Gareth, Neve, Audrey and Simon ... my friends.

And last, but not least, at the top of the list, my ever-loving Jo for being in my life ... cue song.

First published in 2018 by New Holland Publishers

London • Sydney • Auckland

131–151 Great Titchfield Street, London WIW 5BB, United Kingdom

1/66 Gibbes Street, Chatswood, NSW 2067, Australia

5/39 Woodside Ave, Northcote, Auckland 0627, New Zealand

newhollandpublishers.com

A record of this book is held at the British Library and the National Library of Australia.

ISBN 9781921024733

Group Managing Director: Fiona Schultz

Publisher: Alan Whiticker

Project Editor: Liz Hardy

Designer: Andrew Davies

Front cover photo: Geoff Hales

Production Director: James Mills-Hicks

Printer: Toppan Leefung Printing Limited

10 9 8 7 6 5 4 3 2 1

Keep up with New Holland Publishers on Facebook

facebook.com/NewHollandPublishers

Go to www.glennshorrock.com

for all tour dates and recording information.

PLASTIC SWORDS + TOMMY GUN WATER PISTOLS
DADS ACCIDENT KNOCKING LADY DOWN
RAN AWAY TO AUSTRALIA
EMMIGRATION FIRST THOUGHT WAS
N.Z. BUT QUOTA FULL
SO MELBOURNE BECAME DESTINATION
SS ORCADES LEFT TILBURY
AUG 20? JOHN, NAN, + MAD
SAY GOODBYE

IMMIGRATION OFFICER IN LONDON WHO
INTERVIEWED DAD WAS HAROLD HOLT !!?:
~~DAD~~
SHORROCKS LUCK ENOUGH TO BE
GIVEN OWN 4 BERTH CABIN, LUCK OF
THE DRAW? ALTHOUGH IT WAS SITUATED
ON 'Z' DECK JUST OVER PROPELLOR SHAFT
SO NOISE+ VIBRATION TOOK SOME
GETTING USED TO AS DID NO PORT HOLE
ENGLAND DISAPPEARED INTO NIGHT
AND IN MORNING BEGAN ROUGH CROSSING
OF BAY OF BISCAY
STOP AT GIBRALTAR FIRST STEP
ON 'FOREIGN SOIL' FOR ME, WALKED
UP ROCK OF GIB MET 'FAMED
BARBARY APES
ONWARD ACROSS MED TO NAPLES (SEE NAPLES
'& DIE")